Media Ethics

Other Books in the Current Controversies Series

| Media Ethics

Julia Bauder, Book Editor

GREENHAVEN PRESS
A part of Gale, Cengage Learning

Detroit • New York • San Francisco • New Haven, Conn • Waterville, Maine • London

GALE
CENGAGE Learning

Christine Nasso, *Publisher*
Elizabeth Des Chenes, *Managing Editor*

© 2009 Greenhaven Press, a part of Gale, Cengage Learning

Gale and Greenhaven Press are registered trademarks used herein under license.

For more information, contact:
Greenhaven Press
27500 Drake Rd.
Farmington Hills, MI 48331-3535
Or you can visit our Internet site at gale.cengage.com

Articles in Greenhaven Press anthologies are often edited for length to meet page requirements. In addition, original titles of these works are changed to clearly present the main thesis and to explicitly indicate the author's opinion. Every effort is made to ensure that Greenhaven Press accurately reflects the original intent of the authors. Every effort has been made to trace the owners of copyrighted material.

Cover photograph reproduced by permission of Dennis Kitchen/Stone/Getty Images.

LIBRARY OF CONGRESS CATALOGING-IN-PUBLICATION DATA

Media ethics / Julia Bauder, book editor.
    p. cm. -- (Current controversies)
    Includes bibliographical references and index.
    ISBN-13: 978-0-7377-4144-5 (hardcover)
    ISBN-13: 978-0-7377-4145-2 (pbk.)
    1. Journalistic ethics. I. Bauder, Julia.
    PN4756.M35 2008
    174'.907--dc22
    2008031436

Printed in the United States of America
1 2 3 4 5 6 7 12 11 10 09 08

Contents

Chapter 1: Do Journalists Go Too Far to Get Information for Their Stories?

Yes: Journalists Should Use Ethical Means to Get Stories

Chapter 2: What Information Should Journalists Include in Their Reporting?

Chapter 3: How Do Ethical Concerns Affect the Media's Coverage of War and Terrorism?

Chapter 4: When Should Journalists Abandon Neutrality?

Foreword

By definition, controversies are "discussions of questions in which opposing opinions clash" (Webster's Twentieth Century Dictionary Unabridged). Few would deny that controversies are a pervasive part of the human condition and exist on virtually every level of human enterprise. Controversies transpire between individuals and among groups, within nations and between nations. Controversies supply the grist necessary for progress by providing challenges and challengers to the status quo. They also create atmospheres where strife and warfare can flourish. A world without controversies would be a peaceful world; but it also would be, by and large, static and prosaic.

The Series' Purpose

The purpose of the Current Controversies series is to explore many of the social, political, and economic controversies dominating the national and international scenes today. Titles selected for inclusion in the series are highly focused and specific. For example, from the larger category of criminal justice, Current Controversies deals with specific topics such as police brutality, gun control, white collar crime, and others. The debates in Current Controversies also are presented in a useful, timeless fashion. Articles and book excerpts included in each title are selected if they contribute valuable, long-range ideas to the overall debate. And wherever possible, current information is enhanced with historical documents and other relevant materials. Thus, while individual titles are current in focus, every effort is made to ensure that they will not become quickly outdated. Books in the Current Controversies series will remain important resources for librarians, teachers, and students for many years.

In addition to keeping the titles focused and specific, great care is taken in the editorial format of each book in the series. Book introductions and chapter prefaces are offered to provide background material for readers. Chapters are organized around several key questions that are answered with diverse opinions representing all points on the political spectrum. Materials in each chapter include opinions in which authors clearly disagree as well as alternative opinions in which authors may agree on a broader issue but disagree on the possible solutions. In this way, the content of each volume in Current Controversies mirrors the mosaic of opinions encountered in society. Readers will quickly realize that there are many viable answers to these complex issues. By questioning each author's conclusions, students and casual readers can begin to develop the critical thinking skills so important to evaluating opinionated material.

Current Controversies is also ideal for controlled research. Each anthology in the series is composed of primary sources taken from a wide gamut of informational categories including periodicals, newspapers, books, U.S. and foreign government documents, and the publications of private and public organizations. Readers will find factual support for reports, debates, and research papers covering all areas of important issues. In addition, an annotated table of contents, an index, a book and periodical bibliography, and a list of organizations to contact are included in each book to expedite further research.

Perhaps more than ever before in history, people are confronted with diverse and contradictory information. During the Persian Gulf War, for example, the public was not only treated to minute-to-minute coverage of the war, it was also inundated with critiques of the coverage and countless analyses of the factors motivating U.S. involvement. Being able to sort through the plethora of opinions accompanying today's major issues, and to draw one's own conclusions, can be a complicated and frustrating struggle. It is the editors' hope that Current Controversies will help readers with this struggle.

Introduction

Media ethics seems like a simple, never-changing concept built on eternal principles: tell the whole truth in one's stories, don't embellish, and be fair and unbiased, to name a few examples. But in fact the ethical values of journalism are always changing. Even such a seemingly fundamental value as "never fabricate any part of a story" has not always been seen as critical to good journalism.

Throughout the nineteenth century, few people saw newspaper stories that were partially or entirely made up as an ethical problem. Many newspapers, especially the inexpensive "penny papers," saw themselves as entertaining their audiences rather than informing them, and reporters and editors knew that an exaggerated or completely fabricated story was often more entertaining than reality.

Possibly the purest example of a made-up story in American newspaper history is what later became known as the Great Moon Hoax. In 1835 the *New York Sun* ran an incredibly popular series of articles describing life that had supposedly been discovered on the moon via a new, powerful telescope. The *Sun* claimed that these articles were based on discoveries reported in the *Edinburgh Journal of Science* (an actual journal, but one that had not published a new issue for two years), and the stories mimicked the scientific tone of such a journal. In technical language, the articles described the supposed inhabitants of the moon, including tiny bison-like creatures, blue animals that looked like goats, and something that seemed to be a cross between an orangutan and a bat. The hoax was so convincing that even some scientists fell for it, and it was so popular that the *Sun*'s circulation more than quadrupled when the stories ran.

Some of the other New York newspapers that competed with the *Sun* unmasked the hoax within a few weeks. These competing newspapers tried to use the hoax to discredit the *Sun*, although without much success. A few sticklers for accuracy in reporting also complained about being misled, but they were in the minority. Even Sir John Herschel, the real and very famous scientist to whom the made-up discoveries were attributed, saw the hoax as a harmless amusement for the gullible. The paper's readers seemed equally unconcerned about the stories' falseness: The *Sun*'s circulation continued to rise even after the hoax was unmasked.

Today, fabricating stories is one of the cardinal sins of journalism—although it is a sin that is still frequently committed. Every year or so it is discovered that a contributor to a newspaper or a magazine made up some part of a story. Jayson Blair was forced to resign from the *New York Times* in 2003 when it was discovered that he had fabricated and plagiarized dozens of stories. A photographer at the *Toledo (OH) Blade* resigned in 2007 after digitally altering a number of photographs. The *New Republic* had to retract stories written by a soldier serving in Iraq after it could not corroborate some aspects of those stories. Yet now, every time a major fabrication is uncovered it becomes a scandal, with the editors of the duped publication frequently offering abject apologies and sometimes even resigning. An editor and a reporter today would have a very difficult time holding on to their jobs if they knowingly perpetrated a hoax as audacious as the Great Moon Hoax.

Although the ethical status of fabricating stories seems to be settled today, many other ethical questions that once seemed decided are now in flux. Is it ethical for journalists to go undercover and lie about being reporters to get information? Should the media continue its longstanding practice of not naming alleged rape victims? Should journalists continue to be neutral among all sides when they write their stories, or should they abandon their neutrality and stand up for the side that they feel is morally correct? These are some of the questions debated by the authors in *Current Controversies: Media Ethics*.

CHAPTER 1

Do Journalists Go Too Far to Get Information for Their Stories?

An Overview of Journalistic Ethics

Marianne Jennings

Marianne Jennings is an award-winning newspaper columnist and radio commentator, director of the Joan and David Lincoln Center for Applied Ethics, and professor of legal and ethical studies at Arizona State University, Tempe.

Print and broadcast media should be guided by five values: honesty, independence, fairness, productiveness, and pride.

A lawyer by training and a newspaper columnist by avocation, I teach ethics at a business school. My career choices have made me realize that attorneys, businessmen, and journalists wrestle with the same ethical concerns, though journalists face the greatest challenge. They not only have to decide whether to follow a code of ethics personally, but whether it should apply to the stories and subjects they cover professionally.

When the News Is Fictional

Journalists often regard ideas about right and wrong as old-fashioned and outmoded. Some fail to live up to high ethical standards. Consider this admission by a famous reporter: "Tales of lawsuits no court had ever seen involving names no city directory had ever known, poured from me. Tales of prodigals returned, hoboes come into fortune, families driven mad by ghosts, vendettas that ended in love feasts, and all of them full of exotic plot turns involving parrots, chickens, goldfish, serpents, epigrams, and second-act curtains. I made them all up."

Was it *New Republic* associate editor Stephen Glass? He was fired in May, 1998, for making up out of whole cloth half a dozen articles and fabricating portions of more than 20 others. Or was it *Boston Globe* columnists Patricia Smith and Mike Barnicle? It was revealed in June, 1998, that they were allowed to keep on writing for years after their editors suspected that they were making up people and events. Or was it CNN's star producer April Oliver? She was booted from the network in July, 1998, after airing a false story claiming that the U.S. military used nerve gas in Laos.

Actually, it was Ben Hecht, the legendary newspaperman who began his career at the *Chicago Journal*. In 1910, as a cub reporter, he confessed to making up news stories and was suspended for a week. Hecht was never again to write fiction as a journalist, but he did go on to do so as a highly successful novelist, playwright, and Hollywood screenwriter. You may remember seeing the original play or one of the many movie versions of his most famous script, "The Front Page," a 1928 comedy about—what else?—reporters caught up in their own lies. Journalists are tempted to fiddle with the truth because they need to write sensational stories that will sell newspapers. The "scoop" was everything back in 1910, and remains so today.

As an ethics professor, I have found that those who rely most on written codes of conduct are the most unethical among us.

In 1947, Henry Luce, the founder of *Time, Life*, and *Fortune* magazines, commissioned a report which concluded that the press wields enormous power for its own ends; propagates its own opinions at the expense of opposing views; allows advertisers to dictate editorial content; resists social change; prefers the superficial and sensational; endangers public morals; invades privacy; is dominated by one socioeconomic class; and interferes with the open marketplace of ideas.

Luce was livid when he read this report, fearing that Congress would step in and take control. Congress refrained, however, and the nation still has freedom of the press, as outlined in the First Amendment.

A newspaper publisher was once confronted by a prominent businessman who complained, "I don't like what your reporters and editors have been saying about my company." The publisher replied, "I'm sorry, but I can't control these people." We should not want to control "these people" through government regulation, but we should expect them to deal honestly and fairly with their subjects, and hold them responsible in the courts and the marketplace.

The Fourth Estate

Eighteenth-century British conservative statesman Edmund Burke called the press the "fourth estate," implying that it was as important and influential as the three estates, or branches, of government. His contemporary and ideological foe, the French philosopher François-Marie Voltaire, came up with what (as it was later paraphrased) became the rallying cry of the press: "I disapprove of what you say, but I will defend to the death your right to say it." Both men would have agreed with former Pres. John Adams when he wrote in 1815: "If there is ever to be an amelioration of the condition of mankind, philosophers, theologians, legislators, politicians, and moralists will find that regulation of the press is the most difficult, dangerous, and important problem that they have to resolve. Mankind cannot be governed without it, nor at present with it."

First and foremost, you should define the values that you hold most dear.

A free press is necessary for the effective functioning of our republic. Yet, it is also an invitation to abuse.

Given all the scandals that have occurred recently, journalists have been trying to agree upon a professional code of ethics. The American Society of Newspaper Editors and the Society of Professional Journalists have published their own versions. Both are well-crafted and feature many sound ideas, but err by focusing less on journalists' conduct than on the "public's right to know." In other words, they say a lot about the rights and very little about the press' responsibilities.

As an ethics professor, I have found that those who rely most on written codes of conduct are the most unethical among us. They want a fancy document certifying their integrity that they can wave around, but do not want to be bound by it. It is no wonder that one of America's most popular journalists in the early to mid 20th century, *American Mercury* founder H.L. Mencken, called ethical codes for journalists "flapdoodlish and unenforceable."

"Jurassic Park" Ethics

Many journalists are content to practice what I call "Jurassic Park" ethics. In this movie, a wealthy businessman finds a way to genetically engineer DNA so as to revive extinct species. He uses this ingenious process to create a theme park full of live dinosaurs. He stands to make untold millions, but his lawyers are afraid that the park is unsafe. To allay their fears, the developer invites a team of scientists to investigate. One, a mathematician, states his doubts, which go far beyond the question of safety: "The problem that I have with what you have done here is that you spent so much time asking whether you could do this that you forgot to ask whether you should do this." Unless journalists grapple with the "should" question, written codes of ethics are meaningless.

Let me explain further by relating an incident that happened in my classroom. A student asked me, "Would you embezzle $1,000,000 from your employer if your mother needed it to pay for a lifesaving operation?" My response was an emphatic "No!" He was upset and cried, "Why, you heartless wench! No wonder I'm getting a C in this class." It never occurred to him that there were other ways to phrase the question. If he were to ask, "Would you raise the money for your mother's operation?," my answer would be "Yes!" If he were to ask, "Would you pledge everything you owned for your mother's operation?," my answer would again be "Yes!"

That student, like a number of ethically challenged journalists today, doesn't seem to realize the importance of value-based decision-making. First and foremost, you should define the values that you hold most dear. I propose that journalists be guided by five important values. (I have borrowed them from novelist Ayn Rand, but I could have easily found them in the writings of many thinkers.)

Honesty

Honesty. Journalists should not invent stories, "fudge" facts, or foster false impressions. This last provision may be the most critical. My son Sam would never tell an outright lie, but he is willing to tell less than the whole truth. His second-grade teacher put his name on the chalkboard if he failed to follow the rules. My husband and I asked him every day after school, "Did you get your name on the board?," and he would answer truthfully. When he was in the third grade, we asked the same question, and the answer was always "No." We were thrilled that his conduct had been so exemplary.

Then we learned from his teacher that she had changed the policy. Names no longer were written on the chalkboard, but on index cards. We went home from parent-teacher conferences to confront our son: "Sam, you lied to us. You told us that you were good." He replied earnestly, "No, I did not lie to you. You asked me if I got my name on the board, and the answer was always 'No.'" My husband looked at me and sighed. "Dear," he said, "we are raising a president."

Likewise, it is wrong to exaggerate the truth. In 1992, NBC's "Dateline" presented an investigative report on General Motors [GM] trucks. There is no question that there was a defect in the gas tanks, but the show's producers secretly detonated incendiary devices in a staged crash. A popular car magazine exposed the scandal, though it was not until GM spent $2,000,000 on a full-scale investigation that NBC admitted any wrongdoing. Even then, network president Michael Gartner insisted that the segment was "fair and accurate."

This is deeply troubling, especially since television is the primary source of news in the world today. As syndicated columnist Richard Reeves points out, it is a form of mass media that is fraught with ethical problems, since millions of viewers believe that the camera doesn't lie.

Independence

Independence. Journalists should avoid conflicts of interest. One such conflict occurred in 1998, when the Walt Disney Company, which owns Capital Cities/ABC Inc., killed an ABC television news magazine series on lax security and pedophilia in amusement parks. Another transpired when ABC newswoman and celebrity interviewer Barbara Walters ran a flattering profile of composer Andrew Lloyd Webber just before his musical "Sunset Boulevard" opened on Broadway in 1997. What Walters failed to disclose and what the *New York Post* revealed the following week was that she had invested $100,000 in the show. Ironically, Walters responded to the charge like the typical businessman who is so often the target of "20/20" ambush interviews: "How could you ever think that I would compromise my integrity for money?"

Fairness

Fairness. While it could be argued that the truth by definition is fair, 19th-century British poet William Blake was right when he wrote, "A truth told with bad intent/Beats all the lies you can invent."

The "truth" in the profile of Chief Justice William Rehnquist in the Jan. 25, 1999, issue of *People* was meant to wound: "Among the controversies [surrounding Rehnquist] were reports that covenants on his house in Phoenix and a vacation home in Vermont prohibited their resale to racial or ethnic minorities." A parenthetical note followed: "(Rehnquist claimed he had been unaware of the covenants.)" The obvious implication was that the Supreme Court is led by a closet racist.

As the author of a real estate law text, I can assure you that there are very few properties in the U.S. that don't have racial covenants hidden somewhere in their history. Such covenants were declared unconstitutional in the 1950s, but to require property owners or clerks to strike them physically from all the land records in the nation would be an immense undertaking. We don't have the resources or the funds to do so, and the idea is plain silly anyway since the covenants have been declared invalid. Furthermore, covenants often appear only in chains of title and not in the deeds. So, property owners are not likely to know that they even exist.

Fairness is also endangered by personal bias. Journalists may agree with the individuals, organizations, and causes they are covering, so it may be hard for them to report anything negative. Similarly, they may disagree and find it hard to say anything positive.

Scan any newspaper for stories about, say, the environment, and you will discover that many journalists are predisposed to consider environmental activists the "good guys" and oil company presidents and loggers the "bad guys." Or watch all the television news specials about pesticides, food additives, breast implants, nuclear power, and global warming. Reporters are reputed to be natural-born skeptics, but they almost never challenge alarmists on these important issues.

Productiveness

Productiveness. Journalists should do their own homework. The secret of success in any field is hard work, but in journalism, it is also the key to getting the story right. Some of the best reporters are often referred to sneeringly as "junkyard journalists," but that's because they go where no one else is willing to go and they check up on the little leads that appear to be dead ends.

Value-based decision-making is lacking in the modern media. As consumers of the news, we ought to do everything in our power to remind journalists that it should be paramount.

Doing your work means that you do not accept the word of somebody else; you check the facts yourself. That's what Rod Decker, a local television reporter, did in Salt Lake City in 1998. He broke one of the biggest stories of the year when he discovered that bribery and widespread corruption influence the way Olympic sites are selected. Although most members of the community were uncomfortable with his revelations and some became hostile, Decker persisted.

Then there is the enterprising, diligent, and courageous reporting of *Newsweek* veteran Michael Isikoff. As one source admits, "Years from now, when we look back on the Clinton impeachment scandal, Michael Isikoff's name will be stamped on the story." Despite his editors' strong disapproval, he painstakingly investigated allegations of sexual misconduct on the part of the President. He did so as a serious reporter, not a tabloid sleazehound, yet he is branded as such by Clinton supporters.

Isikoff has no regrets, having stated that he is glad that he pursued the truth. This puts me in mind of an old adage that his critics would do well to heed: "The truth is violated by falsehood, but outraged by silence."

Pride

Pride. Permit me once again to use an example from my own life. Years ago, when I was working in the U.S. Attorney's Office, we did not have word processors. One of the secretaries finished making final copies of a 75-page brief for an appellate case. At the last minute, I discovered a typographical error. I went to the senior attorney and said, "This is not my fault. I corrected the typo on the last draft, but the secretary missed it." He looked at me and asked, "Does it have your name on it?" When I replied that it did, he said matter-of-factly, "Then it is your mistake."

It doesn't matter how many people help a journalist on a story. When it appears in print or on the air with his name on it, he has to take responsibility for it. This is a hard lesson that even veteran journalists have difficulty learning. Remember the dishonest CNN report I mentioned earlier about alleged use of nerve gas in Laos? The reporter who presented that story to the American public was Peter Arnett. While he was not fired, Arnett was reprimanded by the cable network after insisting that he hadn't really done any real reporting at all—he had just read the script that was handed to him. Nevertheless, he had allowed his name to appear in the credits for a story that turned out to be false. Shouldn't he have held himself accountable?

Clearly, value-based decision-making is lacking in the modern media. As consumers of the news, we ought to do everything in our power to remind journalists that it should be paramount.

Journalists' Use of Deception to Get Information Is Ethically Questionable

Howard Kurtz

Howard Kurtz is a journalist with the Washington Post. *He is also the host of the CNN program* Reliable Sources *and the author of several books about the media, including* Reality Show: Inside the Last Great Television News War.

Ken Silverstein says he lied, deceived and fabricated to get the story.

But it was worth it, he insists. Those on the receiving end don't agree.

As Washington editor of *Harper's* magazine, Silverstein posed as Kenneth Case, a London-based executive with the fictional Maldon Group, claiming to represent the government of Turkmenistan. He had fake business cards printed, bought a London cellphone number and created a bogus Web site— all to persuade Beltway lobbying firms to pitch him on representing Turkmenistan.

"For me to deny, or try to shade the fact that I tricked them would be stupid," Silverstein says. "Obviously we did. If our readers feel uncomfortable, they're free to dismiss the findings of the story."

Says *Harper's* Editor Roger Hodge: "The big question in our mind was whether anybody was going to fall for it."

They did. According to *Harper's*, executives at the Washington firm APCO Worldwide laid out a communications plan that included lobbying policymakers—possibly including a trip for members of Congress—and generating "news items." Senior Vice President Barry Schumacher told Silverstein the firm could drum up positive op-ed pieces by utilizing certain think tank experts. The proposed fee: $40,000 a month.

There was no discussion of anything illegal. On human rights issues, Schumacher said there were bound to be "isolated incidents that look bad, and it's up to the communications company to figure out a way to be honest about them, to react and put them in the proper perspective." He told Silverstein that "we live up to the spirit and letter of the law" in registering as foreign agents, but would provide "minimal information."

Amateurish and Unethical

APCO has written a letter of complaint to *Harper's*, and company spokesman B. Jay Cooper says Silverstein's approach was "pretty amateurish." The firm had not yet decided to represent Turkmenistan, and it was Silverstein who was "being unethical," he says. But Silverstein says APCO pursued him hard and expressed disappointment at being turned down.

Another Washington firm, Cassidy & Associates, asked for at least $1.2 million a year and touted a proposed trip to Turkmenistan for journalists and think tank analysts. "We are surprised that a reporter would go to such extraordinary lengths to gather information in such a deceptive way that really isn't all that new or interesting," the company says in a statement.

"What bothers me most," says APCO's Cooper about the story in the July [2007] issue, "was there was never a moment where he unveiled himself and asked us to comment on anything we did wrong, because we didn't do anything wrong. They never called us to say, 'You got punked.'"

Says Silverstein, noting the magazine's long lead time: "These guys are professional spinners, and I didn't feel like giving them six weeks to lie their way out of the story." He says his piece exposed how lobbying firms try to manipulate public opinion.

"If you want to weigh my ethics in making up a firm against the ethics of agreeing to represent and whitewash the record of a Stalinist dictatorship, I'm pretty comfortable with that comparison."

Hodge says the caper is part of "a long history of sting operations" by journalists. But that undercover tradition has faded in recent years. No newspaper today would do what the *Chicago Sun-Times* did in the 1970s, setting up a bar to entrap crooked politicians. Fewer television programs are doing what ABC did in the 1990s, having producers lie to get jobs at a supermarket chain to expose unsanitary practices. NBC's "Dateline" joins in stings against child predators, but by tagging along with law enforcement officials.

The reason is that, no matter how good the story, lying to get it raises as many questions about journalists as their subjects.

Journalists Should Not Pay Police and Other Groups to Help Create Dramatic Stories

Deborah Potter

Deborah Potter is the executive director of NewsLab, an organization dedicated to improving television and radio journalism.

The "To Catch a Predator" series on "Dateline NBC" has been a smash hit for the network's news division since it launched . . . , drawing a substantial audience and public praise for bringing sex offenders to justice. But the program's tactics have always been controversial, and now they've landed NBC in court. The charge is breach of contract, but the complaint paints a picture of a program willing to cross ethical lines to win ratings.

Former "Dateline" producer Marsha Bartel, who worked at NBC for more than 20 years, was let go [in] December [2006] just a few months after being promoted to sole producer of the "Predator" series. Bartel says the company told her she was being dropped in a general round of layoffs. While there's no question that NBC has been downsizing, Bartel believes she was forced out because she complained to her supervisors that the "Predator" series repeatedly violated the standards of ethical journalism.

Paying for News?

NBC has disclosed that it pays an advocacy group, Perverted Justice, to set up the "Predator" sting operations featured on 10 installments of "Dateline" [as of August 2007]. The group's volunteers pose as young teens in Internet chat rooms, looking for adults interested in having sex; when they arrange to meet, the network's hidden cameras are waiting.

Deborah Potter, "Over the Line," *American Journalism Review*, August 2007. Reproduced by permission of American Journalism Review.

NBC insists it's not paying for news, but Bartel's lawsuit alleges the payments violate the network's own standards against conflict of interest. "Contrary to NBC Policies and Guidelines, NBC unethically pays Perverted Justice to troll for and lure targets into its sting," the lawsuit says, "thereby giving it a financial incentive to lie and trick targets." Bartel says that targets sometimes are "led into additional acts of humiliation (such as being encouraged to remove their clothes) in order to enhance the comedic effect of the public exposure of these persons."

The program also works closely with police—too closely, according to Bartel. Her complaint says the network provides police with video equipment and tapes so they can record the arrests they make for NBC to air. She also alleges that NBC pays or reimburses law enforcement officials to participate in the stings "in order to enhance and intensify the dramatic effect of the show." Do these practices make the "Dateline" staff an arm of law enforcement or turn the police into journalists? Either way, they're a bad idea.

A Step Too Far

To be fair, reporters and editors enhance dramatic or comic elements of a news story all the time, by choosing what information to include and where to place it. But paying or tricking participants in a story to intensify the drama or comedy crosses the line. This isn't "Candid Camera." "Dateline" is supposed to be a news program.

There are plenty of other worthwhile stories going begging for airtime while "Dateline" tracks perverts.

It's also true that undercover journalism is a noble tradition that has exposed serious wrongdoing in the past. "Dateline" itself has used hidden cameras to reveal fraud at car dealerships and child labor violations. But those stories had wide impact, and the video was necessary to prove the case. On that basis, "Predator" doesn't measure up.

For the Greater Good?

"Predator" reporter and host Chris Hansen defends the program and its tactics. In promoting his new book based on the series, Hansen has bragged that of the more than 200 men charged in the investigations, only one has been found not guilty. "I think . . . it's for the greater good," he told NPR's [National Public Radio's] "Talk of the Nation." But some of the cases are not going to court. A Texas district attorney threw out 23 arrests from a "Dateline" sting as inadequate for prosecution. One sting target in Texas fatally shot himself last fall [2006] as officers forced their way into his house, while NBC cameras stood by outside. Hansen says he doesn't feel responsible for the man's death, and he sees nothing wrong with paying Perverted Justice. He compares those payments to the contracts NBC signs with retired generals and FBI agents who comment on the news. But that's a stretch of Rose Mary Woods proportions.[1] The generals aren't setting up wars for NBC to cover.

In a statement responding to Bartel's lawsuit, NBC says it has been transparent about its reporting methods. "Although the reports have been subject to some controversy, audience reaction has been overwhelmingly positive." That's great for NBC's bottom line, but it doesn't justify the way the program operates.

Sensationalism over Substance

No one's suggesting that the would-be predators exposed by "Dateline" are anything other than scummy. But did the network really need to produce 10 programs to make that point

1. Rose Mary Woods was Richard Nixon's secretary who testified in the Watergate coverup investigation that she inadvertently erased eighteen minutes of a taped conversation between Nixon and an aide. Further investigation showed Woods would have had to physically stretch out backwards over her shoulder several feet to hit the recorder as she claimed.

over and over again? All the attention suggests the country is crawling with these creeps, but statistics don't support that. Besides, there are plenty of other worthwhile stories going begging for airtime while "Dateline" tracks perverts.

"Dateline" has done some excellent work; its documentary about a first-year schoolteacher in Atlanta won a Peabody award [in 2007]. It was compelling television, focusing on systemic problems that affect millions more children than Internet predators. But it wasn't sexy and aired just once, in August, when audiences are traditionally low.

Yes, viewers may prefer to watch "humilitainment" like "Predator" instead of a meaningful investigation. But that's no reason to let your news division produce it and pretend it's a documentary.

Journalists Should Testify Against Sources Who Leak Classified Information to Them

Seth Leibsohn and Andrew C. McCarthy

Seth Leibsohn is a fellow at the Claremont Institute, a think tank that advocates for limited government and strong national defense. Andrew C. McCarthy is the director of the Center for Law and Counterterrorism at the Foundation for Defense of Democracies.

Since the War on Terror began, all sectors of the American public have been called upon to do their duty to help aid the war effort. For those opposed to any military action (or war) at all, the best we could hope for from our citizenry was some form of the Hippocratic Oath: at least do no harm. And the American people, by and large, have risen to their duties of citizenship. One sector has, however, behaved miserably: the American media. They have disclosed, published, and broadcast to the world national security secrets from NSA [National Security Agency] surveillance programs to Treasury Department funds-tracking programs and they have outed allies who helped us hold high-value terrorist detainees such as Khalid Sheikh Mohammed.

A New Privilege

For this behavior has a single member of the press been investigated, much less prosecuted? No. Instead, they have given themselves Pulitzer Prizes. And this week [October 15–19, 2007], the House of Representatives has approved legislation that would give them something even more valuable: a new privilege, to be recognized in federal law, allowing them *not* to testify against those who have broken the law by giving them classified national-security intelligence. With this privilege, the media, unlike the rest of us, can now skirt a core obligation of citizenship: the duty to provide testimony when they witness crimes. Indeed, even if they aid and abet certain crimes, our lawmakers would provide them cover.

Even more ardently than most clubs, the American press circles the wagons when its members are criticized. Alas, because we get our information from the media, it matters a great deal when they are deeply self-interested. That self-interest—if not balanced by an equally effective force—cements into conventional wisdom. That is what has happened as freedom of the press has been debated over the last several years, against the backdrop of the high-profile Valerie Plame Wilson leak investigation, in which the only person who went to jail was a reporter, Judith Miller, who defied a subpoena.

An Unneeded Privilege

Correction of the conventional wisdom is badly needed. One might have thought House Republicans, who have exhibited great concern about wartime leaks of national-defense information, would have provided it. To the contrary, they've gone along for the ride, ludicrously suggesting that the press is "under siege"—notwithstanding that newspapers teem with leaks, classified or not, and that Ms. Miller needn't have gone to jail, as she held the key to her cell door the entire time (and ultimately was released when she did what all Americans are obliged to do: honor a lawful subpoena).

Here is what the media does not tell you: 99.9 percent of the time, if not more, journalists are not hampered in the slightest. Justice Department guidelines, which are rigorously enforced, forbid prosecutors and investigators from issuing subpoenas to compel them to surrender their sources. The government pays great deference—far more than the law requires—to the vital role the media plays in a functioning democracy.

There are, nevertheless, two other types of situations. They occur rarely, but when they do there is no public interest served in insulating the journalists from the obligations of citizenship.

Journalists as Witnesses

The first is when a member of the press witnesses a crime. Let's say a reporter happens to be standing on line in a bank when it is robbed. It would be ridiculous to suggest that the reporter's mere status as a journalist should relieve him or her, unlike the other citizens on line, of the obligation to testify as a witness to the robbery.

The First Amendment is not a license to violate the law.

The media may not like this, and the politicians and public officials who leak to them surely don't like it, but unauthorized disclosures of information in government files is a crime. Government officials with security clearances take a solemn oath to keep classified information confidential. Leaking it is not only dishonorable; it is a crime. Moreover, even when information in government files is not classified, officials can be prosecuted—and jailed for up to ten years—under a federal statute that bars the theft of public money, property and records (Section 641 of Title 18, U.S. Code).

That is, a reporter who receives such a leak witnesses a crime every bit as serious—and sometimes more serious— than the journalist who happens to be in the bank when it is robbed. Government officials who leak information can severely compromise our national security, as we have seen only too frequently in recent years. People can die as a result of such leaks. It makes no sense to make them even more difficult than they already are to investigate.

The public interest in having available the testimony of all citizens takes precedence over the journalist's interest in protecting sources.

The establishment media's response to such arguments is bogus. They claim that "whistleblowers" who want to reveal government corruption or incompetence should be encouraged to come forward. But they already are. Government agencies have internal reporting mechanisms and vigilant, independent inspectors general who investigate claims of waste, fraud and abuse—and who ultimately report to the public without disclosing information that would harm the nation or infringe on privacy concerns. No government official has to go to the media to get the truth out, and most leakers are not good-faith whistleblowers; they tend, instead, to be disgruntled losers of internal policy arguments or insiders currying favor with the press.

Journalists as Criminals

One other situation is even more rare and it cries out even more forcefully against "shield" protection for journalists. It occurs when a reporter is potentially complicit in a crime. For example, a federal statute (Section 798 of Title 18, U.S. Code) expressly makes it a crime to *publish* signals intelligence—a category that would include, for example, the NSA's terrorist surveillance program exposed by the *New York Times* in 2005. The espionage act (Section 793) more generally proscribes the disclosure of "information relating to the national defense which information the possessor has reason to believe could be used to the injury of the United States or to the advantage of any foreign nation(.)" This at least arguably applies to the press.

The First Amendment is not a license to violate the law. The prosecution of a journalist would be a very momentous step, one that should be approached with the greatest of caution. But questioning journalists about which government officials are leaking information that can so badly damage national security should be a no-brainer—especially during wartime and under circumstances where the enemy has already accomplished one devastating strike against the homeland and desperately seeks a reprise. It is simply mind-boggling that Congress would take what is very likely *criminal* behavior and turn it into *immunized* behavior—encouraging more top-secret disclosures and putting all of us at greater risk.

Finally, making matters even worse, there is ambiguity in the House legislation regarding who is a journalist. That means much of the new media—including the very bloggers who have been nothing short of heroic in both exposing media bias and getting facts to the American people when the mainstream media does not or will not—would likely not be protected under this legislation. Not if they are part-timers like the "Power Line" or "Little Green Footballs" bloggers . . . or us. In other words, those who have rolled up their sleeves to help the war effort in their spare time will receive no protection while those employed by billion-dollar media corporations who have exposed anti-terror programs will have a brand new level of protection.

The Public Interest

The Supreme Court has wisely held that the public interest in having available the testimony of all citizens takes precedence over the journalist's interest in protecting sources. This is as it should be. That reasonable principle is the basis of the current system. It is a system, in which, far from being under siege, reporters enjoy broad freedom to investigate and report; yet, in exceedingly rare instances, they may be questioned about crimes they may have witnessed and investigated for crimes they may have committed. It would be extremely foolish to upset that balance.

Journalists Should Not Report Unsubstantiated Allegations Based on Anonymous Online Comments

Eric Alterman

Eric Alterman is a professor of journalism at the City University of New York and the author of several books, including What Liberal Media? The Truth About Bias and the News.

There is a specter haunting American journalism; well, dozens actually, but today's specter is the purposeful abuse of the anonymous website comments board. In the past, when a journalist, or even a partisan, wished to attribute a quote to an individual or an organization, it was necessary to obtain some form of evidence that the person being quoted actually existed. No longer. Thanks to the proliferation of e-mails, instant messages and Internet message boards, our most august journalistic institutions are now quoting people who may well be imaginary. Worse, they may have assumed a phony identity for nefarious personal or political purposes.

Unverified Information

The problem has arisen in a variety of contexts of late. When discussing reactions to the news that Bob Dylan appears to have borrowed lyrics from nineteenth-century Confederate Henry Timrod, the *New York Times* quoted an anonymous denizen of a Dylan web fan forum complaining in a juvenile and malicious fashion as a counterpoint to the more learned quotations from genuine Dylan scholars. Who was the guy? Who knows? He didn't even have a name. The Bobster's reputation may have suffered microscopic degrees of damage, but the primary casualty was the *Times*'s reputation for veracity. Similarly, when the *Washington Post*, in one of its periodic sex panics, printed the salacious instant messages of Representative [Mark] Foley and two former Congressional pages, the article noted that "attempts by the *Post* to contact the two former pages were unsuccessful." Nor did the paper reach Foley. Given that almost anyone can fake an IM exchange, to go to press with such damning words whose authenticity is unverified is recklessness itself. (Remember the good old days of the "Watergate rule," which required two corroborating sources for the publication of information based on anonymous sources? That went out the window with Monica Lewinsky's blue dress.)[1]

Anti-Semitic Comments

To see how easily this lazy practice can be exploited, we need look no further than a [2006] article in the *New York Post*. The story, according to its author, Maggie Haberman, was fed to her by aides to Joe Lieberman's senatorial campaign and accused the liberal organization MoveOn.org of promoting anti-Semitism on its message boards. Posters on MoveOn's ActionForum had written of "media-owning Jewish pigs" and "Zionazis" and called the Senator "Jew Lieberman." The story contained quotations from the Anti-Defamation League's Abe Foxman taking MoveOn to task for the message board's "hateful content." In what could have been mere coincidence, I suppose, the story, which was also covered by the Moonie-owned *Washington Times*, was quickly seized upon by Lieberman supporters like Marshall Wittman of the Democratic Leadership Council [DLC] and William Kristol of the *Washington Post*, the *Weekly Standard*, Fox News, etc. Writing on his Bull Moose blog, Wittman asked, "Shouldn't lefties ask themselves why the anti-Semitic haters are attracted to their sites?" and wondered "why Democratic leaders continue to collude with the anti-

1. Lewinsky's semen-stained dress was sought as evidence in the impeachment trial of President Bill Clinton.

Semitic appeasing left." In a widely reprinted *Wall Street Journal* column provocatively titled "Anti-Judaism," Kristol took up this same theme and concluded, "Jews are under attack. And no one seems very concerned. Liberal Jews are more concerned about Mel Gibson than (Iranian President Mahmoud) Ahmadinejad."

How can mainstream media organizations maintain that they hold themselves to higher standards than the ... blogosphere when they ape its most irresponsible practices?

In fact, none of the people reporting, discussing or pronouncing on the MoveOn comments had any idea who made them or why. It would have been easy, for instance, for a Lieberman supporter to post the comments and then complain to the campaign's friends in the [media mogul Rupert] Murdoch and Moonie empires, feigning the kind of shock, *shock* Captain Renault made famous in *Casablanca*. And shouldn't it be obvious that anonymous posters on a public bulletin board do not represent anyone or anything but their own silly little minds? When critic Lee Siegel donned his sock puppet to praise himself and attack the character of those who questioned his brilliance on *The New Republic*'s [TNR] comments board, no one blamed the magazine for Siegel's miasmic *mishigas*, since its editors acted quickly and suspended him. And Siegel was actually employed by *TNR*; the morons who posted on MoveOn may not even exist.

When I took the apparently unthinkable journalistic step of contacting the organization itself to discover what it knew about the incident, I learned that the postings were deleted immediately after MoveOn was informed of them. Many of the organization's key staff members, including its executive director, Eli Pariser, and communications director, Jennifer Lindenauer, are proud Jews and take no less offense at such things than, say, neocon pundits. Even the censorious Foxman, who ran to the media to complain without first talking to anyone at MoveOn about the postings, admitted that the organization had acted appropriately and that the incident was now "resolved satisfactorily."

Low Standards

The attempt to blame MoveOn for these illiterate scrawls is about as credible as blaming a presidential candidate for graffiti near a campaign stop. That Kristol would employ so slender a reed to slander a liberal organization is hardly surprising; this is, after all, a man who admiringly quotes his father Irving's kind words for Joe McCarthy.[2] But Wittman's stance is more puzzling. Leaving aside that his own recent employment by a genuine lunatic anti-Semite, [TV evangelist] Pat Robertson, leaves him on rather thin ice, Wittman cannot have forgotten how his friend and former employer [U.S. senator from Arizona] John McCain was undone by the same kind of unsourced slander by the [George W.] Bush forces in South Carolina in 2000. What's more, Wittman is now employed by the DLC, which may not like MoveOn.org but should at least be respectful of its 3.2 million likely Democratic voters. Nevertheless, when I e-mailed Wittman to ask if he had reconsidered his blog post, he politely replied that he had not. Too bad.

Ultimately, however, it's the journalistic questions that loom largest: How can mainstream media organizations maintain that they hold themselves to higher standards than the Drudge-driven political blogosphere when they ape its most irresponsible practices? Time for another blogger ethics panel, perhaps?

---

2. McCarthy, a U.S. senator from Wisconsin in the 1950s, accused almost everyone in government and the media of being a Communist sympathizer, ruining many reputations in the process.

Undercover Reporting Is a Legitimate Way to Do Investigative Journalism

Ken Silverstein

Ken Silverstein is the Washington editor for Harper's Magazine.

Earlier this year [2007], I put on a brand-new tailored suit, picked up a sleek leather briefcase and headed to downtown Washington for meetings with some of the city's most prominent lobbyists. I had contacted their firms several weeks earlier, pretending to be the representative of a London-based energy company with business interests in Turkmenistan. I told them I wanted to hire the services of a firm to burnish that country's image.

I didn't mention that Turkmenistan is run by an ugly, neo-Stalinist regime. They surely knew that, and besides, they didn't care. As I explained in [the June 2007] issue of *Harper's Magazine*, the lobbyists I met at Cassidy & Associates and APCO were more than eager to help out. In exchange for fees of up to $1.5 million a year, they offered to send congressional delegations to Turkmenistan and write and plant opinion pieces in newspapers under the names of academics and think-tank experts they would recruit. They even offered to set up supposedly "independent" media events in Washington that would promote Turkmenistan (the agenda and speakers would actually be determined by the lobbyists).

All this, Cassidy and APCO promised, could be done quietly and unobtrusively, because the law that regulates foreign lobbyists is so flimsy that the firms would be required to reveal little information in their public disclosure forms.

Ethics Complaints

Now, in a fabulous bit of irony, my article about the unethical behavior of lobbying firms has become, for some in the media, a story about my ethics in reporting the story. The lobbyists have attacked the story and me personally, saying that it was unethical of me to misrepresent myself when I went to speak to them.

That kind of reaction is to be expected from the lobbyists exposed in my article. But what I found more disappointing is that their concerns were then mirrored by *Washington Post* media columnist Howard Kurtz, who was apparently far less concerned by the lobbyists' ability to manipulate public and political opinion than by my use of undercover journalism.

Today . . . it's almost impossible to imagine a mainstream media outlet undertaking a major undercover investigation.

"No matter how good the story," he wrote, "lying to get it raises as many questions about journalists as their subjects."

Decline of Undercover Journalism

I can't say I was utterly surprised by Kurtz's criticism. Some major media organizations allow, in principle, undercover journalism—assuming the story in question is deemed vital to the public interest and could not have been obtained through more conventional means—but very few practice it anymore. And that's unfortunate, because there's a long tradition of sting operations in American journalism, dating back at least to the 1880s, when Nellie Bly pretended to be insane in order to reveal the atrocious treatment of inmates at the Women's Lunatic Asylum on Blackwell's Island in New York City.

In the late 1970s, the *Chicago Sun-Times* bought its own tavern and exposed, in a 25-part series, gross corruption on the part of city inspectors (such as the fire inspector who agreed to ignore exposed electrical wiring for a mere $10 payoff). During that same decade, the *Chicago Tribune* won several Pulitzer Prizes with undercover reporting, and "60 Minutes" gained fame for its use of sting stories.

Today, however, it's almost impossible to imagine a mainstream media outlet undertaking a major undercover investigation. That's partly a result of the 1997 verdict against ABC News in the Food Lion case. The TV network accused Food Lion of selling cheese that had been gnawed on by rats as well as spoiled meat and fish that had been doused in bleach to cover up its rancid smell. But even though the grocery chain never denied the allegations in court, it successfully sued ABC for fraud—arguing that the reporters only made those discoveries after getting jobs at Food Lion by lying on their resumes. In other words, the fact that their reporting was accurate was no longer a defense.

Coziness Between Reporters and Subjects

The decline of undercover reporting—and of investigative reporting in general—also reflects, in part, the increasing conservatism, and cautiousness, of the media, especially the smug, high-end Washington press corps. As reporters have grown more socially prominent during the last several decades, they've become part of the very power structure that they're supposed to be tracking and scrutinizing.

Chuck Lewis, a former "60 Minutes" producer and founder of the Center for Public Integrity, once told me: "The values of the news media are the same as those of the elite, and they badly want to be viewed by the elites as acceptable."

Undercover Reporting Is Needed

In my case, I was able to gain an inside glimpse into a secretive culture of professional spinners only by lying myself. I disclosed my deceptions clearly in the piece I wrote (whereas the lobbyists I met boasted of how they were able to fly under the radar screen in seeking to shape U.S. foreign policy). If readers feel uncomfortable with my methods, they're free to dismiss my findings.

Yes, undercover reporting should be used sparingly, and there are legitimate arguments to be had about when it is fair or appropriate. But I'm confident my use of it in this case was legitimate. There was a significant public interest involved, particularly given Congress' as-yet-unfulfilled promise to crack down on lobbyists in the aftermath of the Jack Abramoff scandal.[1]

Could I have extracted the same information and insight with more conventional journalistic methods? Impossible.

Public Support for Stings

Based on the number of interview requests I've had, and the steady stream of positive e-mails I've received, I'd wager that the general public is decidedly more supportive of undercover reporting than the Washington media establishment. One person who heard me talking about the story in a TV interview wrote to urge that I never apologize for "misrepresenting yourself to a pack of thugs . . . especially when misrepresentation is their own stock in trade!"

I'm willing to debate the merits of my piece, but the carping from the Washington press corps is hard to stomach. This is the group that attended the White House correspondents dinner and clapped for a rapping Karl Rove [outspoken White House aide]. As a class, they honor politeness over honesty and believe that being "balanced" means giving the same weight to a lie as you give to the truth.

I'll take Nellie Bly any day.

---

1. Abramoff was a powerful D.C. lobbyist who pled guilty to corrupt practices that bilked millions from his clients in the early 2000s.

Journalists Are Right to Report Classified Information That Is Leaked to Them

Christine Tatum

Christine Tatum is a journalist with the Denver Post. *She has also served as president of the Society of Professional Journalists.*

Regardless of whether you think journalists use too many anonymous sources, it's hard to argue that they don't need to promise confidentiality sometimes.

Anonymous Sources

Many of the biggest investigative stories of our age have been based in part on information shared with a reporter by someone who wanted to keep his or her identity a secret. Anonymous sources handed over the Pentagon Papers and unmasked the culprits behind Watergate and Enron. They have outed some of the nation's worst corporate polluters. They have helped inform Americans' debates about the Iraq War, the proliferation of nuclear weapons and global warming.

Yes, sources almost always have an agenda when they speak up, but sometimes they have information of vital interest to the general public and much to lose if they're caught passing it along. If journalists can't protect their sources' identities, you will be much less informed about the world.

Currently, 49 states (Wyoming is the only unenlightened one) have shield laws or operate under court rulings that grant journalists and their sources a "privilege" much like those afforded to lawyers and their clients, and therapists and their patients. This protection applies only to local and state cases, not federal ones.

Lately, federal prosecutors have dragged too many journalists into court, flaunting subpoenas for notes, work product and recollections of private conversations. The feds' arrogant insistence that journalists should be compelled to act as arms of law enforcement undermines free speech, a free press and an informed citizenry.

The Federal Shield Law

Journalists need a federal shield law. Thankfully, one is scheduled for reintroduction Wednesday [May 2, 2007,] in Congress. The Free Flow of Information Act of 2007 has bipartisan support in the House and Senate. The bill's sponsors include Reps. Mike Pence (R-Ind.) and Rick Boucher (D-Va.), and Sens. Richard Lugar (R-Ind.) and Christopher Dodd (D-Conn.). All four have fought for a federal shield law for a couple of years, arguing that transparency is good for democracy even if it exposes politicians to more scrutiny.

Among the bill's provisions:

- The federal government could not compel a person covered by the shield to provide testimony or produce documents without first showing the need to do so by a "preponderance of evidence."

- Journalists can be compelled to reveal the identity of confidential sources when the court finds it necessary to prevent "imminent and actual harm to national security" or "imminent death or significant bodily harm." Journalists also may be compelled to identify a person who has disclosed trade secrets, health information or nonpublic personal information of any consumer in violation of current law.

- People covered by the shield would be those "engaged in journalism." Journalism is defined as "the gathering, preparing, collecting, photographing, recording, writing, editing, reporting or publishing of news and information for dissemination to the public." The bill does not explicitly protect bloggers, but to the extent a court determines they are engaged in the practice of journalism, they are likely to be shielded.

Care with Anonymous Sources

Even with the protection of a federal shield law, journalists should use anonymous sources sparingly and take great care to explain to the public why a source's identity needs to remain secret. More Capitol Hill reporters should insist their conversations are on the record. Newsrooms should tighten rules regarding the use of anonymous sources, which undermine the credibility of the news and leave journalism with black eyes at the hands of more reporters than we have the space to name here.

A federal shield law won't end journalists' abuse of anonymous sources, and it won't end prosecutorial witch hunts. It will, however, help the public have access to important information, and that, in the end, is what really matters.

Anonymous Sources Are Sometimes Necessary in Journalism

Stephen Engelberg, Interviewed by Russ Baker

Stephen Engelberg has been a journalist with several publications, including the New York Times *and the* Portland Oregonian. *Russ Baker is a contributing editor with the* Columbia Journalism Review.

R*uss Baker: Has the use of unattributed information changed over the course of your career?*

Stephen Engelberg: I think the pendulum has now swung against it. But it's hard to measure. I came in covering the CIA—that was my first beat. I actually never used named sources.

Never?

Hardly ever. Anyone who talks about classified documents can go to jail. I can honestly tell you I never quoted anyone on the record about a classified piece of information. And I published many classified pieces of information.

Why has the pendulum swung against anonymity, and is this generally a positive development?

We in the industry are under attack as we have never been on issues of credibility. Some of these attacks are warranted. There have been some very well-publicized mistakes and meltdowns of news organizations. But one of the things that critics have fastened onto is the problem of anonymous sources. And to be honest with you, I think it's overblown. I don't have a problem with anonymous sources. I think the problem is poor editing, poor reporting, poor standards, incomplete stories, stories that tell only one side. That aggravates people. That is hurting our credibility.

Anonymity Policy

I Nexised [searched the Nexis online archives] the phrase 'condition of anonymity' for a recent sixty-day period. For The New York Times, *I got 229 hits. For* The Oregonian, *I got two. What's* The Oregonian's *policy?*

We are a paper that is very reluctant to run anonymously sourced material in the news pages. And that's a good thing. But we should not have that prevent reporters from using anonymously sourced materials to gather information. It's a big difference. The fact that you're going to allow someone to go off the record in the course of gathering news may help you get somewhere that you couldn't otherwise get. You may use what you get anonymously to leverage on-the-record confirmation, acknowledgment, whatever.

Sources who are not named, whether anonymous or not, affect the direction of every article.

Is there any controversy over that?

There is. There are people who think that, somehow, having standards equates with never letting people speak off the record. I've heard some younger reporters say: 'I'm very careful; nobody goes off the record with me.' And I say that's not necessarily a good sign. If you're able to get all the scoops you think you should through that method, great, but I doubt you are.

Types of Anonymous Sources

Let's talk about the different levels of unnamed sources.

First of all, sources who are not named, whether anonymous or not, affect the direction of every article. You go and get an interview on the record, and a guy gives you a perfect idea for a story, you go out and pursue it, and you execute it to perfection. But then his quote wasn't quite right, so you use somebody else's quote. He doesn't appear in your story. And yet he's had an extraordinary influence on the direction of the story. That's one level of anonymity. The second level is somebody who anonymously tells you something—'Don't get me involved with this, but Joe Jones has been phonying up his campaign contribution list, and you should look into Joe Jones.' If you then go look at him and find five named sources, but you never name the source who sent you, that is also a form of anonymity. And I think that happens all the time.

Okay. Let's talk about the classic anonymous sourcing, where we quote or paraphrase an unidentified but clearly present source. What's okay and what isn't?

There are orders of magnitude. *The New York Times* for years said they did not allow anonymous pejorative: 'A senior administration official says John Smith is a crook.' That was generally not allowed. But that kind of stuff did start to creep in, pre-Jayson Blair. Even worse, they allowed a lot of anonymous praise: 'The president is just so decisive, you can't believe the way he handled himself in that crisis.' In a funny way, that's as pernicious for the reader as the anonymous pejorative.

So what material, appropriately, should we be attributing to unidentified sources?

Things that are factual: How many troops have been sent to New Orleans? Did the president sign the emergency order on Monday or on Tuesday? You could use that, absolutely. It's not opinion. If you had a document, you could find out if it's true.

Let's say you have a source telling you, not for attribution, a negative story about a powerful person. You believe it to be true, because it is consistent with what you already know and with the direction the facts are headed, and because you have found the source reliable in the past. Can you use that?

Now you go and confront the named person, and say, 'This is what I've heard, and I want you to respond on record.' And if that person says to you, 'That is complete bullshit, this did not happen,' I would be very reluctant to use an unnamed accuser against a named individual.

National Security Reporting

Compare your experiences as an investigative editor at the Times, *which has been relatively free with granting anonymity, with your experience at* The Oregonian, *which has not.*

They're not analogous. The work we do [at the *Oregonian*] is investigative work that does not involve national security, that does not involve exposing classified information to public view. Also, we have in Oregon a very favorable public records law, and are able to obtain access to original documents.

I wonder if in fact The Oregonian *were going after the same stories as the* Times, *if it were on the same playing field, might it not then be just like the* Times?

Well, one of two things would happen. We would either find ourselves loosening our rules, or we would find ourselves ceding stories to the competition. I do not believe under our sort of basic guidelines that *The Oregonian* would have a very easy time with national security stories. In fact, there have been times where we have used anonymous sources, especially on some terrorism cases, because we decided the value of the information outweighed our extreme reluctance to use sources that way.

When your reporters have anonymous sources, do you ask them who they are?

Yes.

And they tell you?

Yes, they do. That was a change for me. At the *Times*, before Jayson Blair, no one ever routinely asked that question. When I was running national security stories, I certainly did not routinely ask that question. I often asked about what kind of person was providing the information. How do they know this? What's their access? On a routine story, I don't think an editor at *The New York Times* would be particularly curious as to which State Department official was talking. I think now they're more curious.

Named sources lie, too, believe me.

Judith Miller

Speaking of which, you were Judith Miller's editor for a while, including when she was working on pre-9/11 terrorism stories. What do we learn about the strengths and weaknesses of anonymous sourcing from her work?

From the pre-9/11 stuff she did on Al Qaeda, you certainly could see that she was tapping into people in the government who felt that not enough was being done. I had a fair idea who they were, and a fair idea of why they felt the way they felt. They had specific reasons that motivated them to talk to us. That's an example where anonymous sourcing can be useful.

And her post-9/11 and Iraq WMD [weapons of mass destruction] reporting?

I was not on deck for most of the controversial stories. There is one I edited, where we had a named source, the famous defector story in the fall of 2001.[1] But there the problem wasn't anonymity. Named sources lie, too, believe me.

Reporting Without Anonymity

What are some great stories that you were able to do without granting anonymity?

---

1. Miller was introduced by exiled Iraqi leader Ahmad Chalabi's group to a man who claimed to have personally worked on renovations of secret WMD facilities. His claims proved false. In 2005, Miller went to jail for refusing to name her source for a leak that revealed the identity of a secret CIA agent.

Two years ago [in 2003], we did an investigation of a child death on an Indian reservation here [in Oregon]. That is an extraordinarily difficult reporting environment. That is a culture where people do not talk about death, where it's sacrilegious to say the name of people who have died. Nonetheless my reporters put in literally months and months building relationships out there, and people went on the record. People were so upset at the rate of childhood deaths that they were willing to talk to this white newspaper about the most intimate tribal details. We could have done that story more quickly if we'd been willing to use anonymous sources. It took a long time to get people on the record. So there's an investment of time, which is money in this business, in a time of diminishing resources. Every year it's going to get harder to do. But we did it.

Then there was the Pulitzer finalist series and follow-up stories on the government's losing battle against the growing illicit use of methamphetamines.

That's a perfect example. Our work there has been very much driven by our own analysis. We did not use one anonymous source—we killed ourselves, I mean killed ourselves, to build our own model of what we believed was the total Mexican domestic consumption of pseudoephedrine [which is used to make both cold medicine and meth] in Mexico. Rather than rely on an anonymous source and calling it a day, we went and bought market research data from an international company, and when that wasn't sufficient, we started calling all the supermarket chains and major pharmaceutical companies in Mexico, and, shockingly, one of them gave us their figures for pseudoephedrine sales in all their stores. It always takes longer if you do it that way.

A Necessary Tool

One of the two stories with anonymous sources that The Oregonian *ran recently was also about methamphetamine. It quoted an unidentified State Department official. Did you okay that?*

Yes, I did. It was a kind of classic Washington thing. The source was acknowledging a very significant thing, but was not going to go on the record. My first desire was that we would get the spokesman to say it, but he gave a vanilla response. So I felt that we would be depriving our readers of what the State Department really thought. I kind of held my nose; I wasn't real happy about it, but I did approve that one.

Overall, though, you see anonymity as a necessary journalistic tool.

I think that if you go back to the modern history of journalism, through Watergate, [famed investigative journalist] Sy Hersh's work, and fifty other things you or I could name, without the anonymous source, we're in deep trouble.

CHAPTER 2

What Information Should Journalists Include in Their Reporting?

Overview: The Debate over When to Minimize Harm and When to Tell the Whole Truth

Fred Brown

Fred Brown retired in 2002 after working at the Denver Post *for more than thirty-eight years. He is a former president of the Society of Professional Journalists (SPJ) and has served as chairman of the SPJ's ethics committee.*

Minimize Harm. It's one of the four major sections of the SPJ Code of Ethics. It's also a major factor in moral reasoning and ethical decision-making.

Many ethical decisions, in journalism and elsewhere, are a struggle between doing one's duty and being responsible about the consequences of that action.

The important thing is to have that debate—either with yourself or preferably with colleagues—and to ask the right questions. A key pair of those questions is this: Who gets hurt if we tell this story? And does the benefit to the public of knowing that truth outweigh that harm?

The heavyweight in this balancing act is the truth. Telling the truth is a journalist's overriding duty. Considering the consequences is a tempering element—a smaller element, but nonetheless an important one.

In the simplest terms, minimizing harm requires being sensitive to the consequences of what you do as a journalist.

"Recognize that gathering and reporting information may cause harm or discomfort," the Code of Ethics says, and remember that "pursuit of the news is not a license for arrogance."

Before the Code of Ethics was revised in 1996, it didn't say much about minimizing harm. Years ago, we were more confident in our righteousness. But while the older SPJ codes of ethics don't actually use the words "minimize harm," they do include some evidence of sensitivity.

The 1984 version is an interesting document. This Code of Ethics has one section, out of six, labeled "ethics." It's all about conflicts of interest—the principles that are now part of the Code's "Act Independently" section. Of course, there's much, much more to ethics than merely avoiding conflicts of interest.

There's another section in that 1984 Code called "fair play." Parts of it correspond to the "Minimize Harm" and "Be Accountable" sections of today's Code. It says, "Journalists at all times will show respect for the dignity, privacy, rights and well-being of people encountered in the course of gathering and presenting the news." Journalists shouldn't "pander to morbid curiosity," it says, but should "make prompt and complete correction of their errors."

The "Fair Play" section represents about one-sixth of that 1984 Code. By contrast, "Minimize Harm" is nearly a quarter of today's Code. Add the "Be Accountable" provisions, and you've got close to a third of the whole thing.

Show Compassion

There is some sentiment in the profession that journalists shouldn't fret about consequences. It makes them timid. Throw it all out there and let come what may. Tell the story and run.

That attitude gives ammunition to journalism's critics, and it helps to explain dwindling trust. Civic journalism's response was to try to show the public that journalists do care, and to pay more attention to readers' and viewers' wants. The 1996

Code revision, with its inclusion of "Minimize Harm," and "Be Accountable," was in part an effort to recognize that new sensitivity.

"Minimizing harm" means letting your humanity show through. Show a little compassion for the people who are affected by what you write. Remember that, for many people, being part of a story is a rare, even once-in-a-lifetime experience. They live with the consequences of what you've written long after you've moved on to other stories.

The Media Should Not Widely Publicize School Shootings and Suicides

Loren Coleman

Loren Coleman is a researcher who studies ways to prevent suicides and school shootings. He is the author of The Copycat Effect: How the Media and Popular Culture Trigger the Mayhem in Tomorrow's Headlines.

A pattern underlies many of the events we hear about in the news every day. But the pattern is not openly discussed on your cable news network, over your twenty-four-hour news radio station, or in your newspaper. It is either overlooked or ignored.

The pattern is called the "copycat effect." It is also known as "imitation" or the "contagion effect." And what it deals with is the power of the mass communication and culture to create an epidemic of similar behaviors.

The copycat effect is the dirty little secret of the media. That doesn't prevent the media from calling the various epidemics of similar behaviors the "copycat phenomenon," often for shock impact. But, curiously, their use of the phrase seems to put a distance between the events and the reporting media, and allows them the stance that implies *they are not part of the problem*. But they are.

The Werther Effect

Sociologists studying the media and the cultural contagion of suicidal behaviors were the first to recognize the copycat effect. In 1974, University of California at San Diego sociologist David P. Phillips coined the phrase *Werther effect* to describe the copycat phenomenon. The name Werther comes from the 1774 novel *The Sorrows of Young Werther* by Johann Wolfgang von Goethe, the author of *Faust*. In the story, the youthful character Werther falls in love with a woman who is promised to another. Always melodramatic, Werther decides that his life cannot go on and that his love is lost. He then dresses in boots, a blue coat, and a yellow vest, sits at his desk with an open book, and, literally at the eleventh hour, shoots himself. In the years that followed, throughout Europe, so many young men shot themselves while dressed as Werther and seated at their writing desks with an open copy of *The Sorrows of Young Werther* in front of them that the book was banned in Italy, Germany, and Denmark.

Though an awareness of this phenomenon has been around for centuries, Phillips was the first to conduct formal studies suggesting that the Werther effect was, indeed, a reality—that massive media attention and the retelling of the specific details of a suicide (or, in some cases, untimely deaths) could increase the number of suicides.

The August 1962 suicide of Marilyn Monroe presents a classic modern-day example of the Werther effect. In the month that followed it, 197 individual suicides—mostly of young blond women—appear to have used the Hollywood star's suicide as a model for their own. The overall suicide rate in the U.S. increased by 12 percent for the month after the news of Monroe's suicide. But, as Phillips and others discovered, there was no corresponding decrease in suicides after the increase from the Marilyn Monroe–effect suicides. In other words, the star's suicide actually appeared to have caused a whole population of vulnerable individuals to complete their own deaths, over and above what would be normally expected. This is the copycat effect working with a vengeance.

Car Crashes and Suicides

Before the appearance of the Internet and cable news, the significance of stories in newspapers, on the radio, and via broadcast television news could be tracked rather well. In a 1979 study on imitation and suggestion, Phillips found an increase in the rate of automobile fatalities immediately after publicized suicides. The more publicity the suicide story received, the higher the automobile fatality rate. As might be expected, the motor vehicle fatalities were most frequent in the region where the suicide story was publicized. More surprising was the fact that younger people dying in vehicle crashes tended to follow reports of younger suicide victims, while older people dying in vehicle crashes tended to follow reports of older suicide victims. This was a striking example of peer group imitation, modeling, and suggestion.

Phillips also managed to get a handle on how long the effect lasts. In examining a two-week period beginning two days prior to the publicized suicide and ending eleven days later, he found that automobile fatalities increased by 31 percent in the three-day period after a suicide was reported in the media. The increase appears to have a lesser seven-day mirror peak as well. . . .

Phillips is quite certain that no other variables are involved in the increase in suicides. "The increase in the suicide rate was not due to the effect of weekday or monthly fluctuations in motor vehicle fatalities, to holiday weekends, or to yearly linear trends," he reported, as his study had taken these other time variables into consideration.

Suicide Clusters and School Shootings

I became interested in the Werther effect as a university-based public policy researcher and author in the 1980s, following an explosion of copycat teen suicides throughout America at that time. In 1987, I wrote the first book on that situation, *Suicide Clusters*, to heighten awareness of the situation at a time when professionals and the media would hardly acknowledge the problem even existed. The book was dedicated to David Phillips for his groundbreaking work, which had been largely ignored by most scholars up to that time.

Suicide clusters of the 1980s would be replaced by the school shootings of the 1990s, almost all conducted by suicidal male youth. The copycat effect had merely shifted its target as the media had shifted its focus. School violence has been around for a long time, but the media-driven contagion of modern school shootings dates back to February 2, 1996, when Barry Loukaitis, a 14-year-old boy in Moses Lake, Washington, killed two students and a math teacher. He ended his rampage by saying, "This sure beats algebra, doesn't it?" Loukaitis had taken the expression directly from the Stephen King novel, *Rage*, which he had really liked and which was about a school killing. Loukaitis said his murderous loss of control was inspired by *Rage*, Pearl Jam's music video *Jeremy*, and the movies *Natural Born Killers* and *The Basketball Diaries*. Unfortunately, the explosive media attention to Loukaitis's school shooting triggered a series of similar events. Today, Stephen King says he wishes he had never written *Rage*.

Glorifying suicide or persons who commit suicide . . . often leads to more suicides.

Evidence from Australia

As the era of school shootings, celebrity suicide copycats, cult deaths, and workplace violence was just beginning, Riaz Hassan, a sociology professor at Flinders University, Australia, essentially replicated Phillips's studies in Australia and confirmed the links between reporting of suicides and further suicides completed. He drew his data from two major metropolitan newspapers, identifying the stories that reported suicides between 1981 and 1990. He then examined the daily suicide rates between 1981 and 1990 and analyzed whether or not the newspaper stories had an effect on the number of suicides in the days following.

Hassan defined the "impact" of a suicide story by noting "the location of the newspaper story, by the size of the newspaper story and headline and by a presence or absence of photographs." Hassan found that the suicide rates of males increased significantly in the three-day period after a suicide, which included the day of publication of high-impact reports and the two subsequent days. . . .

Time for the Media to Wake Up

Until recently the media has kept its head buried in the sand on the subject. News executives only began to pay attention to their role in the copycat effect in September of 1986, when David Phillips and colleague Lundie L. Carstensen published their study "Clustering of Teenage Suicides After Television News Stories About Suicide," in *The New England Journal of Medicine*. Their study concluded that the television news stories actually "triggered" additional suicides among teens. In an editorial in the same issue of *The New England Journal of Medicine*, Dr. Leon Eisenberg said: "It is timely to ask whether there are measures that should be undertaken to limit media coverage of suicide."

Copycats are a consequence of a thoughtless, sensational media.

Interviewed soon after the article was published, David Phillips observed: "It is really up to the news media themselves to decide where it leaves us. Only the media should be involved in the debate. As a native of South Africa, a country without freedom of the press as we know it, I value freedom of the press very highly. I would be very upset if people used my findings in order to suppress news media coverage. But I do think it would be responsible for the news media themselves to bear in mind results of studies like these."

No one is asking the media to stop reporting the news. This is not about censorship. It is not about the right or left, conservative or liberal. It is about looking at how the stories are being presented, how the current approach has backfired and triggered the copycat effect. In essence, the media has to stop using rampage shootings, celebrity suicides, bridge jumpers, and school shootings the way it uses tornadoes, hurricanes, and earthquakes to get people to watch their programs. Human behavior reporting impacts future human behaviors. Copycats are a consequence of a thoughtless, sensational media, and denial and ignorance of the problem will not make it go away.

CDC Recommendations

The media remain undereducated or uninformed about the copycat effect and what they can do to prevent it. As clinical psychologist Madelyn Gould noted in the *American Behavioral Scientist* in 2003, while discussing a recent survey of journalists, "Many reporters did not appreciate the potential for suicidal contagion as a result of newspaper stories. Those who had heard about the phenomenon expressed doubts about its validity."

Despite the atmosphere of media denial and skepticism, attempts have been made to get a handle on the media's propagation of copycats. In 1989 groups of prevention experts gathered to make recommendations to the Centers for Disease Control, beginning with the media guidelines that might help diminish the contagion when reporting suicides. Many of the strategies they proposed apply just as well to all the violent acts of the copycat effect. From those early meetings (of which I was a part), in 1994, Patrick W. O'Carroll, M.D., director of the Office of Program Support of the Centers for Disease Control (CDC) formalized a series of copyright-free government recommendations ("Suicide Contagion and the Reporting of Suicide") that were published and reproduced widely so that members of the media would be aware of them and hopefully follow them. These recommendations pointed out, for example, that certain types of coverage (graphic, photographic, sensational) stimulated copycat suicides, and that responsible mass media might do well to minimize such representations. The guidelines indicated that it was undesirable for the media to present and report how-to descriptions of suicides or describe technical details about the method of suicide. Glorifying suicide or persons who commit suicide, the CDC concluded, often leads to more suicides.

Out of these findings, in 1995 the CDC, the American Foundation for Suicide Prevention, the American Association of Suicidology, and other prevention organizations issued more specific recommendations for the media, noting, for instance, that the language the media used to describe suicides could contribute to "suicide contagion" or copycat suicides. The World Health Organization then adapted many of the recommendations of the CDC, Gould, and others, and came out in the late 1990s with further guidelines aimed at the media. They felt the media could play a proactive role in helping to prevent suicide by acting on many of these recommendations, in addition to listing help-line phone numbers and focusing on messages of sympathy for the grieving survivors.

An Unresponsive Media

Despite hopes that these media guidelines would be rapidly implemented, the reality was otherwise. Suicides are still sensationalized by the media, and suicide clusters continued to occur in this new century from California to Connecticut, and from Maine to Florida. Yet, the worth of such guidelines has been confirmed, unintentionally, by "accidental censorship" events like news strikes. Several studies conducted by suicidologists in the 1980s and 1990s found that age- and gender-linked suicides do decrease during "suicide blackout" periods caused by newspaper strikes. Strict implementation of media guidelines, in a case that verges on censorship, works also. Finding itself in the middle of an "epidemic" of subway suicides in Vienna, Austria implemented media guidelines for suicide news reporting developed by the Austrian Association for Suicide Prevention in 1987. During the first year an immediate significant decline (7 percent) in suicide rates occurred. In the four-year period following the forced removal of suicide stories from the newspapers, the overall suicide rate decreased nearly 20 percent, with an even sharper decline (75 percent) in subway suicides, the specific focus of the media guidelines.

For a while in the wake of the terrorist events of September 11, 2001, when a virtual media moratorium occurred with regard to reporting school shootings and workplace rampages because the mass media concentrated mostly on terrorism and war, the number of copycat incidents of these kinds of rampage shootings dropped to almost zero in the United States. By 2003, however, the media had returned to reporting sensational stories of local violence, again feeding the copycat effect frenzies of the recent past.

Suicides, murder-suicides, and murders—the events that are at the core of the most negative projections of the copycat effect—will remain newsworthy in the eyes of the media in the foreseeable future and will continue to be reported. So what, short of self-censorship, should the media do to halt the contagion of the copycat effect? While the recommendations of prevention experts during the last two decades have applied specifically to suicides, I have generalized them so that they also apply to all forms of violence that fall under the media-driven propagation of the copycat effect.

More Recommendations

Here, then, are my seven recommendations:

1. The media must be more aware of the power of their words. Using language like "successful" sniper attacks, suicides, and bridge jumpers, and "failed" murder-suicides, for example, clearly suggest to viewers and readers that someone should keep trying again until they "succeed." We may wish to "succeed" in relationships, sports, and jobs, but we do not want rampage or serial killers, architects of murder-suicide, and suicide bombers to make further attempts after "failing." Words are important. Even the use of *suicide* or *rampage* in headlines, news alerts, and breaking bulletins should be reconsidered.

2. The media must drop their clichéd stories about the "nice boy next door" or the "lone nut." The copycat violent individual is neither mysterious nor healthy, or usually an overachiever. They are often a fatal combination of despondency, depression, and mental illness. School shooters are suicidal youth that slipped through the cracks, but it is a complex issue, nevertheless. People are not simple. The formulaic stories are too often too simplistic.

3. The media must cease its graphic and sensationalized wall-to-wall commentary and coverage of violent acts and the details of the actual methods and places where they occur. Photographs of murder victims, tapes of people jumping off bridges, and live shots of things like car chases ending in deadly crashes, for example, merely glamorize these deaths, and create models for others—down to the method, the place, the timing, and the type of individual involved. Even fictional entertainment, such as the screening of *The Deer Hunter*, provides vivid copycatting stimuli for vulnerable, unstable, angry, and depressed individuals.

4. The media should show more details about the grief of the survivors and victims (without glorifying the death), highlight the alternatives to the violent acts, and mention the relevant background traits that may have brought this event to this deathly end. They should also avoid setting up the incident as a logical or reasonable way to solve a problem.

5. The media must avoid ethnic, racial, religious, and cultural stereotypes in portraying the victims or the perpetrators. Why set up situations that like-minded individuals (e.g., neo-Nazis) can use as a road map for future rampages against similar victims?

6. The media should never publish a report on suicide or murder-suicide without adding the protective factors, such as the contact information for hotlines, help lines, soft lines, and other available community resources, including e-mail addresses, websites, and phone numbers. To run a story on suicide or a gangland murder without thinking about the damage the story can do is simply not responsible. It's like giving a child a loaded gun. The media should try to balance such stories with some concern and consideration for those who may use it to imitate the act described.

7. And finally, the media should reflect more on their role in creating our increasingly perceived violent society. Honest reporting on the positive nature of being alive in the twenty-first century may actually decrease the negative outcomes of the copycat effect, and create a wave of self-awareness that this life is rather good after all. Most of our lives are mundane, safe, and uneventful. This is something that an alien watching television news from outer space, as they say, would never know. The media should "get real" and try to use their influence and the copycat effect to spread a little peace rather than mayhem.

The Media Should Run Fewer Stories About Urban Crime

Christopher Shea

Christopher Shea is a Washington-based writer. His work has appeared in the Boston Globe, Atlantic, Salon, *and other publications.*

Police in Long Beach, Calif., [in May 2005,] gunned down—on live television—a man who had led them on a high-speed 40-minute car chase which concluded with the driver stumbling out of his car, drawing a gun, dropping it, and seeming to reach for another. Two LA newscasts rode the chase, and the climactic shooting, to dizzying ratings heights in the 5 p.m. time slot. And the star of the grim show was a 37-year-old Hispanic man named Angel Galvan.

Racism and Crime Coverage

After Galvan's on-air death, there was the usual tsk-tsking from media critics about the voyeuristic coverage, followed by a quick return to the "if it bleeds, it leads" school of TV news. But at least one observer in the LA area says the trouble with such spectacles goes beyond mere tastelessness: Local news shows, he argues, are doing nothing less than blocking progress in race relations—and the Federal Communications Commission [FCC] is unwittingly helping them do it.

Obsessive coverage of urban crime by local television stations, UCLA law professor Jerry Kang argued in the *Harvard Law Review* this spring [2005], is one of the engines driving lingering racism in the United States. So counterproductive is local broadcast news, he says, that it is time the FCC stopped using the number of hours a station devotes to local news as evidence of the station's contribution to the "public interest," which has traditionally been a requirement for a broadcast license. (The FCC does not have quotas on how much news must be produced. But Kang points out that the FCC defended its controversial decision in 2003 to loosen ownership rules governing who can own stations on the grounds that the new arrangements would lead to more hours of local news programming.)

Research on Racism

More broadly, Kang's article—titled "Trojan Horses of Race"—is an attempt to jump-start a conversation about race and public policy by drawing on the latest psychological research. That conversation is currently stalled, with predictable divisions. "I don't think most people above college age change their views about how the law should intervene to bring about racial equality," Kang said in an interview. For example, you're either for or against affirmative action and that's that. "What could break this deadlock is not new moral arguments but new information about how racism works."

The new information he has in mind comes from psychological studies of "implicit racism" and how video imagery can trigger or mitigate it. The Harvard social psychologist Mahzarin Banaji, for example, has shown that people who reveal no overt racism (including many people of color) still associate black faces more easily with words like "violence," and white faces with words like "smart."

Local news, with its parade of images of urban criminality, serves as a "Trojan Horse" or "virus" keeping racism alive.

In another study cited by Kang, white and black subjects played the role of a cop in a simulated video game, in which they were forced to make split-second decisions about whether to fire at a suspect on the screen. Both white and black subjects shot unarmed black men more often—mistaking, say, an innocuous wallet for a handgun. Yet another study showed that white test subjects were more likely to favor the death penalty if they watched a news story about a black murderer than if they watched an identical story about a white murderer. (The two "stories" were designed by researchers and differed only in that detail.)

On the other hand, white subjects who take an "implicit racism" test after seeing footage of a respected black figure—like Bill Cosby or Martin Luther King, Jr [MLK]—find that their measure of implicit racism drops significantly.

Proposals for Change

Far from contributing to the public interest, Kang argues, local news, with its parade of images of urban criminality, serves as a "Trojan Horse" or "virus" keeping racism alive in the American mind. And so, with its rules encouraging local-news programs, he writes, the FCC has "unwittingly . . . linked the public interest to racism."

These days, local news is so popular and cheap to produce that stations would almost certainly air it even if the FCC didn't encourage them to. So what's the point of Kang's proposal? And wouldn't the news get even worse if you took away the pretense of public service?

Kang says his ideas could help prompt a national conversation about how local television really could contribute to the public interest. But he also offers two more specific—and radical—proposals. First, since television stations have weaker First Amendment freedoms than those enjoyed by other press outlets (consider the indecency rules they must follow), he asks, why couldn't the FCC recommend a cap for crime coverage of 15 percent per hour? (Kang cites research showing that in one 13-month stretch, coverage of violent crime led LA newscasts 51 percent of the time and took up 25 percent of total newscast minutes.) The question of whether the cap was met would then be considered at license-renewal time.

Kang also floats the idea of having the FCC require stations to run public-service announcements condemning racism throughout the day. The research, recall, suggests that having Denzel Washington and Tiger Woods say such things as "Be Fair. It's what MLK would do," followed by footage of civil rights marches (this is Kang's actual example) would help to disinfect the airwaves contaminated by crime reports on the evening news.

The Public Interest

Even some colleagues who agree that local news is vacuous (or worse) have some doubts about his proposals, to put it mildly. "A ludicrous idea," responds Geoffrey R. Stone, former University of Chicago Law School dean and a First Amendment expert there, via email when asked about the idea of a cap on crime coverage. "That the FCC can regulate the use of [profanity] and Janet Jackson's breast is a far cry from determining what constitutes news."

Yale Law School's Jack M. Balkin, another First Amendment scholar, is more politic but still dismissive. "The goal of the public-interest requirement is to make sure things are included" like children's programming "not that they are taken off the air," he says. "It's a very basic principle."

While it's easy to make fun of Kang's First Amendment-challenged remedies, it's also hard to say he's not onto something in terms of identifying a problem. The authors of the FCC's public-interest standards didn't have in mind footage of running gun battles on LA's freeways. They were thinking along the lines of PBS's "NewsHour with Jim Lehrer." What they got, instead, was "Cops," narrated by better-looking people.

The Media Should Not Publish Details of Sex Crimes Against Minors

Kira Cochrane

Kira Cochrane is the women's editor at the Guardian, *a newspaper based in London, England.*

If you'd been kidnapped at the age of ten and held captive in a tiny cell for eight years, what do you suppose you would want to do immediately after you escaped? Speak to a friendly therapist, perhaps? Spend hours and days sleeping and taking long, hot baths in a comfortable, secure hotel? Or how about sharing all the gory details of your confinement (including as much sexual detail as you could muster) with the world's press?

It is no surprise that the Austrian teenager Natascha Kampusch has chosen to avoid this last route. Yet she has clearly been under huge pressure to reveal all, as evidenced by the pointed letter that she recently released, addressed to "journalists, reporters [and] public opinion". "I would like to say," she states, "that I do not want to and will not answer any questions about intimate or personal details. I will take action against anyone who crosses this line, voyeuristically or otherwise. Whoever tries that should watch out."

Unhealthy Interest

These are hard-headed and heartfelt words. Unfortunately, however, they seem unlikely to stem prurient interest in her story. Because when it comes to young female victims of pae-

Kira Cochrane, "What Natascha Should Not Be Asked," *New Statesman*, vol. 135, September 11, 2006, pp. 20–22. Copyright © 2006 New Statesman, Ltd. Reproduced by permission.

dophiles and sex murderers, the public's appetite for their ordeals seems to be almost insatiable, and is decidedly creepy.

With any murder or kidnap case, there is, of course, every reason to report what happened, to try to unravel basic questions of guilt and logistics. However, the story of Holly Wells and Jessica Chapman, as well as that of Sarah Payne [two ten-year-olds and an eight-year-old who were murdered in the United Kingdom], ran and ran in the press, propelled at least in part by a startling public hunger to know the minutiae of how exactly these girls had been abused.

What parent whose daughter has been killed by a paedophile really wants the sexual details of the crime pored over?

In recent weeks we have also been reminded of the Jon-Benet Ramsey story—possibly the most lurid of them all. The killing of this beauty pageant contestant—a shockingly sexualised six-year-old—was championed by the American supermarket rag the *National Enquirer*, which ran article after article replete with sleazy detail. Again, I have no idea how public speculation about what had happened to her sexually could be in any way instructive.

Torn Parents

In the case of sex murder we can, unfortunately, quite easily imagine the likely details, if we really want to—we don't need them spelled out. But, instead, we dig for information, and our prurient interest puts the parents of these murdered children in a terrible situation. On the one hand, they know that keeping the story in the press piles pressure on the police and the justice system: a good thing when you're intent on a positive verdict. On the other, they must be well aware that widespread interest in their daughter's story has an unwholesome side, at the very least. What parent whose daughter has been killed by a paedophile really wants the sexual details of the crime pored over, their child's terrifying last moments reduced to a weird public titillation?

With the market in weekly real-life magazines booming, each headline on the covers more shocking and salacious, our appetite for these stories seems more pronounced, and more regularly fed, than ever before.

I'm not suggesting that we should always turn away from darkness, horror and evil. Clearly, there are some crimes where rubbernecking is not only acceptable, but essentials—where we have to take a deep breath and look. When Martha Gellhorn reported from the Dachau death camp, for instance, in the days following the end of the Second World War, our interest was justifiable. Reporting every detail in perfect, direct prose, her descriptions of the stinking piles of corpses, of the horrific "experiments" carried out on prisoners, are an ongoing testimony to the worst that human beings can devise: a record of crimes that, as Gellhorn said, should make us feel "ashamed for mankind".

Complicity with Criminals

Yet while these kidnappings and sex murders also make us ashamed for mankind, I'm not sure that prying into the sexual details, over and over, generally tells us anything much at all about the individual criminals—who are usually unerringly oblique. Rather, it tells us something vicious about ourselves.

When people talk about the intense interest in these cases, they often accuse those who eat up the horror of intruding on the parents' grief, making themselves complicit in a tragedy that is not theirs to claim. In fact, our complicity lies elsewhere. Many people are murdered each year, but most of those that the press and public focus on are attractive young women and girls, because, horrifically, we find their cases more sexually compelling.

When it comes to our hunger for these stories, it is not the girls' parents we are complicit with, but the criminal himself. The small, dark corner of our brains that feeds on this information is a tiny reflection of the full-blown sickness of child abusers and murderers.

And, for someone such as Natascha Kampusch, our fervent interest in her experience, our prying and questions and speculation, have the potential to create a second ordeal to rival her first. The only way forward is to do exactly as she has asked. Just leave her well alone.

The Media Should Publish the Names of Alleged Rape Victims

Harry Reynolds

Harry Reynolds is the editorial page editor at the Mattoon, Illinois, Journal Gazette *and the Charleston, Illinois,* Times-Courier.

The Associated Press [AP] has decided to continue to withhold the name of the woman who falsely accused three Duke lacrosse players of rape.

The AP is sticking to the politically correct policy of not identifying victims of sexual assault. Withholding victims' names is not a matter of law, it is a matter of choice on the part of most of the news media.

I think it's a bad choice and flies in the face of the First Amendment. The amendment assures the people's right to know. It does not give the press license to play censor.

Protecting Accusers

Kim Gandy, president of the National Organization for Women, told the AP she hopes the Duke case won't change the media's policy.

"The purpose is not only to protect the person making the criminal complaint—it's to offer some sense of protection for any woman who might need to do so in the future. Once a woman is exposed, regardless of the reason, it has a chilling effect for every other woman."

It also, as resoundingly demonstrated in the Duke case, makes it easier to accuse others of rape—thereby putting them in the spotlight—without the accuser having to worry about being identified by the news media.

For over a year, three Duke students have been terrorized by a district attorney more interested in getting reelection than getting at the truth. And the district attorney Mike Nifong wasn't alone in dispensing judgment before the facts.

Members of the Duke faculty; leaders of the black community; Jesse Jackson and Al Sharpton; and countless commentators and radio talk show hosts piled on.

The three Duke lacrosse players, David Evans, Reade Seligmann, and Colin Finnerty, were accused and lynched by a mob of public opinion.

Nifong referred to the athletes as "a bunch of hooligans." He withheld the results of lab tests showing there was no DNA from the players on the accuser. There was DNA from other men, however.

False Accusations

In declaring the three Duke players innocent, North Carolina Attorney General Roy Cooper decried a "rush to accuse" by a rogue district attorney.

Cooper said the state's investigation into the stripper's claim she was sexually assaulted at a team party found nothing to collaborate her story. The woman is black and attended nearby North Carolina Central University.

Cooper said no charges would be brought against the woman.

Rape . . . should be covered by the news media in the same manner as any other crime.

Things could get real interesting for the AP and other news media still declining to identify the woman if the three exonerated players decide to file a civil suit against the accuser.

If Evans, Seligmann, Finnerty and their families file a multi-million dollar suit against the woman who accused them of rape, would the AP continue to suppress the identity of the woman?

One can easily understand why these young men might want to exact a certain amount of vengeance against the person who nearly destroyed their lives.

They were booted out of Duke and the lacrosse team's season was canceled even before they were tried.

What happened at Duke shouldn't have happened, but it did. And we should all pause and take a lesson from it.

Double Standards

Rape is a horrible crime, but it is still a crime and should be covered by the news media in the same manner as any other crime. Embarrassment does not justify the abandonment of the First Amendment the news media so enthusiastically demands adherence to in crying, "The people want to know!"

The double-standard applied to rape cases drips of hypocrisy.

If anything, the promotion of the notion that rape is an act of violence (which it is) collides with the reality that it is still regarded by some as an act somehow the fault of the victim.

Being an act of violence, its exercise against a victim is clearly the fault of the attacker.

Why then, does the news media, in general, treat rape as the fault of the victim?

In slamming the door on identity, the news media only reinforces the perception that the victim should feel guilty and hide in disgrace.

Protecting the Accused

And what is to be done about situations like the one at Duke, where three young men were treated so shabbily in the court of public opinion, and almost criminally, by a district attorney who played to the crowd rather than the truth?

Should consideration be given to the possibility that, perhaps, the names of the alleged perpetrators in rape cases should be withheld from the public by the news media out of concern for their reputations?

What about the shame they must feel in being publicly accused of a rape they may not have committed? Which was exactly the case with the Duke players.

Why not refuse to publish the identities of people accused of rape?

It shouldn't be difficult. The news media opened the floodgate by withholding the identities of rape victims. Some news media are also beginning to do it in cases involving other crimes.

It's ironic that the news media complains about government withholding information from the public at the same time it plays censor in criminal cases.

We use the First Amendment to justify our emotions, not our reasons.

The Media Should
Not Publish the Names
of Rape Victims

Amanda Paulson

Amanda Paulson is a staff writer for the Christian Science
Monitor.

If, by now, you don't know the name of the woman who accused Kobe Bryant of rape at a Colorado resort June 30,
[2003,] it's probably because you're not interested.

It's certainly not because her identity has been well
shielded.

Spend five minutes on Google, and you'll find not only
the alleged rape victim's name, but her yearbook photos,
phone number, e-mail address, friends—even the address and
phone number of the nurse who examined her afterwards.

So far, the news media, with the exception of California
radio host Tom Leykis, have mostly stuck by policies of withholding names of rape victims—but they've been quick to
give every other personal detail of her life: where she went to
college, the town she lives in, what her house looks like.
They've aired and printed rumors that she was "hospitalized
for her own protection," overdosed on drugs, bragged about
the encounter with Mr. Bryant, and tried out for *American
Idol*. For the past month [July 2003], the media have camped
out at her Colorado home.

The Media Circus

The Bryant case has swiftly become the O.J. Simpson (or Gary
Condit or Lacy Peterson) [all high-profile murder cases] event
of the summer. When Bryant showed up in tiny Eagle, Colo.,

to hear charges against him, reporters nearly outnumbered residents. Photos wrongly identifying Katie Lovell, another Eagle resident, as the accuser were so widely posted online that she went on CNN and Good Morning America last month [July 2003] to set the record straight.

But beyond the media circus—or the question of what actually happened at the Cordillera Lodge and Spa—loom the larger ethical issues involved in sexual-assault cases, particularly ones with such high-profile defendants: What privacy is owed to victims? Is it fair to name the accused but not the accusers? Are personal details off limits? Has the Internet made this type of privacy a relic of the past?

"The celebrity angle, the intense competition, and the Internet have all kind of lined up to create a situation where it makes it very difficult for journalists to remember what their standards are for covering sexual assault," says Kelly McBride, who teaches journalism ethics at the Poynter Institute in Florida.

One of the most consistent standards, held by nearly every media outlet in the country, is to grant rape victims a degree of anonymity. Most began withholding names in the 1970s, as feminist groups stirred awareness of sexual assault and its stigma. The idea is that since rape is such a violation of privacy, and since shame around it lingers, publishing victims' names would add insult to injury—and might dissuade some from filing charges. It's one of few areas where the media voluntarily stays silent.

The Bryant case, however, has revived those questions. Mr. Leykis justified naming Bryant's accuser by saying that, if rape is about violence and not sex, the victim shouldn't have stigma or shame. Others have wondered whether withholding victims' names actually contributes to rape's stigma, cultivating a silent shame. Many have also raised the issue of fairness to the accused: False charges of rape can, after all, ruin a life.

Double Standards

Such arguments often surface in high-profile celebrity cases—a fact that discourages Helen Benedict, author of "Virgin or Vamp: How the Press Covers Sex Crimes." "Terrible double standards come into play," she says.

In the Central Park jogger case, for instance, the media were nearly universal in keeping the investment banker's name out of print. But just two years later, when William Kennedy Smith was accused of raping a woman at a party, that restraint fell like dominoes: First the British tabloids, then *NBC News*, then The *New York Times*, the *San Francisco Chronicle*, and other major papers printed her name. All claimed they were simply following competitors' leads, but Ms. Benedict says that move—as with the Bryant case—was primarily based on who the accused and accuser were.

National surveys show that rape victims' No. 1 concern is people knowing they've been attacked—even ahead of worries about sexually transmitted diseases.

Charles Gay pleads innocent to such inconsistency. The editor and publisher of the *Shelton-Mason County Journal*, in Shelton, Wash., may run the only paper in the country that always prints rape victims' names—no matter their ages.

It's a policy he's been roundly criticized for—and has gone to court to defend—but he stands by it both as a matter of journalistic consistency and for helping erode the stigma of rape. By withholding names, he says, "you are sending the message that we're protecting you because there's something wrong with you."

Others—including a few feminists—agree with him. After the Central Park jogger case, Karen DeCrow, a former president of the National Organization [for] Women, wrote in *USA Today*: "Pull off the veil of shame. Print the name."

Most Against Name Disclosure

But most papers agree that while they'd like to ease shame around rape—and may seek out victims willing to talk—it's too soon to name them all. National surveys show that rape victims' No. 1 concern is people knowing they've been attacked—even ahead of worries about sexually transmitted diseases.

In the Bryant case, privacy questions have grown far more complex than whether to print the accuser's name.

A tougher question is whether concerns about victims' privacy have gotten so extreme as to compromise defendants' rights. After all, being *accused* of rape brings stigma too—a fact not lost on Bryant's supporters. Mr. Gay often asks critics to imagine it's their father or brother or son on trial.

That's the strongest argument for naming victims, says Ms. McBride of the Poynter Institute. But in the end, she concludes, "this is one of the few cases where minimizing harm has overshadowed fairness, and that is because the harm is so great, and so prevalent."

In the Bryant case, privacy questions have grown far more complex than whether to print the accuser's name. Many have noted the hypocrisy of withholding a name while disclosing every other detail—many of which seem designed to discredit her.

Listening to the news has been dispiriting, says Benedict—evidence that little has changed since the days of Mike Tyson and William Kennedy Smith [famous people accused of rape]. The press has "just been doing the same old thing, it's inaccurate legally, it's terribly unfair to her, and it breeds the kind of discussion . . . that's unfortunate," she says. Ultimately, she'd like to see that reflexive analysis deconstructed. "If we want to destigmatize rape, we want to talk about what it really does to people," she says. "Think about how rape is covered in the forum of war. Their credibility is not questioned. Why do we change the rules when it's at home?"

The Media Should Publish the Names of Both Accuser and Accused in Rape Cases

Geneva Overholser

Geneva Overholser teaches at the Missouri School of Journalism. She was formerly an editor at the Des Moines Register *and an ombudsman—an investigator of reader complaints—at the* Washington Post.

In the crime of rape, it is time we named the accuser as well as the accused.

An awful lot of cruelty surrounds the crime of rape. The crime itself, of course, is unspeakably cruel. And the reaction is often cruel, as well. In what other instance are victims so painfully scrutinized? Where else do we see such loathsome insinuations about a victim's character? So many false assumptions? So much ignorance? Cruelty feeds on ignorance. And I have yet to see ignorance effectively addressed by secrecy.

On all the tough problems, from AIDS to teen suicide to drug addiction to priests who abuse children, society has made progress when the truth is told. When real people talk about real experiences. When names are named.

Telling the Whole Story

What fundamental elements of good journalism these are: Getting at issues that most people prefer not be dealt with. And naming names is an essential part of the commitment to accuracy, credibility, and fairness. This practice frequently brings pain to individuals; truth-telling does have its victims. My own view is that recovery from difficult times is, like journalism, abetted by openness and hampered by secrecy. But the larger point is this: Openness serves society as a whole. It serves enlightenment and understanding and progress. And it serves the criminal justice system.

When journalists depart from the commitment to telling the whole story, to naming names, to getting at painful truths, we tread on dangerous ground. With very few exceptions— national security, individual cases in which loss of job or loss of life will clearly ensue—the best journalistic principle is to tell the public what we know. Selecting certain categories of information and seeking to do social work by acting against this principle is dangerous territory. Clearly, we owe children special protection. Beyond that, who of us is wise enough to select—out of all those who would prefer not to have their names in the paper—the winning categories? A general obligation to share the information we have is our surest course.

Treat the woman who charges rape as . . . any other adult victim of crime. Name her, and deal with her respectfully.

Over the decades, however, a consensus emerged that we would make one such choice. We have responded to the eloquent pleas of rape victims and victims' counselors, recognized the cruelty of the stigma of rape, and agreed to keep out of the newspapers and most other mainstream media the names of those who charge others with rape. Most people feel that this is the humane thing to do. I wonder if it has not prolonged the stigma, and fed the underreporting. Certainly, in the past dozen years, we have made progress in reporting on, and understanding, the crime of rape. I am certain that this is in large part due to the courage of women who were willing to come forward and tell their stories. I also wonder if the unfairness of naming the accused and not the accuser has given platform to those who make outsized claims about the number of false charges of rape. And I wonder if shielding the accuser does not inflame still further the cruel search for dirt about her.

Futile Efforts

But here is the new development: As a practical matter, whether shielding rape victims was the right thing to do or not, it no longer makes sense. Newspapers are not—as they once were—the gatekeepers of such information. The culture has changed. Details about the Kobe Bryant accuser are being bandied about by shock jocks and on the Net netherworld. Mainstream media stick to an outdated policy, which has turned into a conceit. This empty posturing produces stories such as the one by the *Orange County Register*, raising questions about the mental stability of the accuser in the Kobe Bryant case—and then intoning: "*The Register* is not identifying the woman because of the sensitive nature of the case." The people who know the woman already know she's the one involved in this case. Meanwhile, much of the nation hears or reads irresponsible charges against her.

The responsible course for responsible media today is this: Treat the woman who charges rape as we would any other adult victim of crime. Name her, and deal with her respectfully. And leave the trial to the courtroom.

The Media Should Not Publish the Names of People Accused of Sex Crimes

Cathy Young

Cathy Young is a contributing editor at Reason *magazine and* Reason.com *and the author of* Ceasefire! Why Women and Men Must Join Forces to Achieve True Equality *and* Growing Up in Moscow: Memories of a Soviet Girlhood.

The charges of sexual assault brought against Los Angeles Lakers guard Kobe Bryant have reignited the debate about the laws and policies that have evolved in the past three decades to protect the privacy of complainants in rape cases—from the practice of withholding the name of the alleged victim in news stories to the legal exclusion of evidence related to her (or his) sexual past.

At first glance, such measures seem fair and humane. Why shouldn't a rape victim be able to seek justice and safeguard her privacy? Why should defense attorneys be allowed to drag a victim through the mud by painting her as a slut who was "asking for it"?

Yet these protections have come under increased scrutiny. Some say that withholding the name of the accuser conveys the message that she is in fact a victim and that the accused is guilty. Even if the man is acquitted or the charges are dismissed, the stigma may linger.

Protecting the name of the accuser may also create an uneven playing field. When a man is charged with a sex crime, other women may come forward to claim that he assaulted them in the past. Under some circumstances, such claims are admissible in court; even if they are excluded, the publicity is likely to compound the damage to the man's reputation. Meanwhile, people who have information that could call the accuser's credibility into question—for instance, that she has previously made false charges of rape—may never even find out that they know the person involved in the case.

Shielding the accuser's identity is not a matter of law but of media policy (though the judge presiding over the Bryant case has given it a legal imprimatur by threatening legal sanctions against media outlets that publicize the accuser's name or image). But questions are also being raised about shield laws that make an alleged victim's sexual history inadmissible in a rape trial.

Exposing an Accuser's History

The last notorious case to raise these issues was that of sportscaster Marv Albert, who was accused by his longtime friend and lover Vanessa Perhach of oral sodomy and assault. At the 1997 trial, Albert's attorneys wanted to bring up Perhach's alleged conduct with other men, particularly men who ended relationships with her—as Albert, who was getting married, was about to do. She had reportedly harassed and threatened a former boyfriend's family, and may have made false accusations of crimes as a form of revenge. A former lover was also willing to testify that biting, on which the assault charge against Albert was based, was a part of her sexual repertoire.

Being sexually assaulted is a terrible ordeal—but so is being falsely accused.

All this testimony, however, was barred from the trial—while a woman who came forward to claim that Albert had sexually assaulted her several years earlier was allowed to take the stand. With the defense's hands tied, Albert pleaded guilty to misdemeanor assault.

In another high-publicity case, Oliver Jovanovic, a graduate student at Columbia University, was convicted in 1998 of sexually assaulting a female student he had met on the Internet. The young woman claimed that Jovanovic tied her up and sexually abused her. The defense argument that the two engaged in consensual bondage was crippled by the trial judge's decision to exclude portions of the e-mail correspondence in which the young woman discussed her interest in, and past experiences with, sadomasochism. The Appellate Division of the New York State Supreme Court subsequently reversed the conviction on the grounds that the shield law was improperly used to exclude relevant evidence.

Honesty Is the Key

When rape shield laws were first enacted, they were a response to truly abusive practices. Just 30 years ago, jurors in rape cases were often formally instructed to consider evidence of "unchaste character" (such as going to bars alone or using birth control) as detracting from the complaint's credibility. But in recent years, even some legal experts who are highly sympathetic to the interests of women—such as Columbia University law professor George Fletcher—have expressed concern that the pendulum may have swung too far against the interests of the accused.

Many feminist groups fiercely resist any weakening of rape shield laws, including a [2003] New Jersey Supreme Court ruling which allows evidence of past sexual contact between the accuser and the accused to be used at trial. Yet feminism should be about equal justice, not just the advantage of women. Women who come forward with charges of rape should not be treated as liars or sluts, but neither should they be given automatic credibility. Being sexually assaulted is a terrible ordeal—but so is being falsely accused.

CHAPTER 3

How Do Ethical Concerns Affect the Media's Coverage of War and Terrorism?

Chapter Preface

Wars are one of the most difficult subjects for journalists to cover well. On the one hand, both readers and journalists agree that wars are topics of critical importance that deserve thorough, in-depth coverage. The public is intensely interested in news about how a war is progressing, and journalists are more than willing to provide that news. On the other hand, there is a general consensus that the public should be shielded from certain aspects of warfare. Journalists are often willing to keep military secrets out of their stories to protect national security; newspapers are wary of running photographs showing bodies blown apart by bombs or bullets. Journalists and their editors put a great deal of time and thought into giving the public all of the information that they need and want without stepping over those lines.

However, the line separating information that the public should have and information that should not be published is not always clear. The case of Sergeant Hector Leija shows the difficulty of determining precisely where this line should be.

On January 28, 2007, a *New York Times* reporter and a photographer who were embedded with the U.S. Army in Iraq went along on a mission with a platoon that included Leija. As the photographer's video camera rolled, Leija and his platoon searched an apartment building in Baghdad for weapons and militants. Then, with the camera still rolling, a bullet fired from the street below came through a kitchen window and struck Leija in the head, mortally wounding him. The cameraman and reporter continued to record the events as Leija was evacuated and as the rest of the platoon huddled in the apartment's living room, waiting for it to be safe to return to the kitchen to collect Leija's gear.

Over the next few days the reporter's story and the cameraman's photographs and video appeared in the *New*

York Times print edition and on its Web site. The story of Leija's death, told in words and images, was poignant, but it was also much more detailed—at times disturbingly so—than is the norm for reporting about combat deaths.

The military, Leija's family, and conservative bloggers reacted fiercely to the graphic nature of the photographs and video. The U.S. military declared that the reporter and photographer had violated the terms of their agreement with the army, which stated that the media could not publish images of dead or dying soldiers without the family's consent. Lt. General Raymond Odierno, who was at that time the commander of the multinational forces in Iraq, wrote a stern letter to the editor of the *New York Times* expressing his displeasure with the reporting. "This story can and should be told," Odierno wrote. However, he continued, "what is disturbing to me personally and, more important, to the family of the soldier . . . is that the young man who so valiantly gave his life in the service of others was displayed for the entire world to see . . . in such a fashion as to elicit horror at its sight."

On the other side, many critics of the war defended the reporting. They argue that voters must hear detailed and vivid stories such as Leija's if they are truly to understand the human costs of the war in Iraq. The *New York Times* also stood by the story. The paper's foreign editor, Susan Chira, said in a statement that the *New York Times*'s reporters "try to write with respect and compassion" for the losses suffered by the families of fallen soldiers. "We believe the article was a portrait of Sergeant Leija's courage under fire and showed how much his men respected and cared for him," Chira wrote.

The debate over Leija's story is just one of many controversies about the media's coverage of America's post-9/11 wars. The authors in the following chapter discuss several of these issues.

The Media's Use of Neutral Labels for Attackers Is Ethical

Christine Chinlund

Christine Chinlund is the ombudsman—the person responsible for investigating complaints from readers and suggesting solutions—at the Boston Globe.

With [the] 9/11 anniversary comes reflection on all that has changed. . . . Even our language has shifted; the word terrorism itself casts a different shadow. It has always, of course, been a powerfully negative label. But post-9/11 the word's potency has multiplied. In the current climate, the terrorist tag effectively banishes its holder from the political arena. More than ever, it condemns rather than describes.

Indeed, newspapers must be doubly careful about how they apply the word. Sparing use is the norm. For example, the Palestinian organization Hamas, whose suicide bombers maim and kill Israeli citizens, is routinely described in the *Globe* and other papers as a "militant," not terrorist, group.

Such restraint infuriates some Middle East partisans (most often, but not exclusively, supporters of Israel) who say it sugarcoats reality and that any group targeting civilians is terrorist. I receive regular demands to, as [one *Globe*] reader put it, "stop misleading readers with terminology that affords terrorists a false degree of legitimacy."

Care with the "Terrorist" Label

What possible reason is there for not unflinchingly applying the word terrorist to any organization or person who targets civilians? It may seem like hair-splitting, but there's a reason to reserve the terrorist label for specific acts of violence, and not apply it broadly to groups.

Christine Chinlund, "Who Should Wear the 'Terrorist' Label?" *Boston Globe*, September 8, 2003. Copyright © 2003 Globe Newspaper Company. Republished with permission of The Boston Globe.

To tag Hamas, for example, as a terrorist organization is to ignore its far more complex role in the Middle East drama. The word reflects not only a simplification, but a bias that runs counter to good journalism. To label any group in the Middle East as terrorist is to take sides, or at least appear to, and that is not acceptable. The same holds true in covering other far-flung conflicts. One person's terrorist is another's freedom fighter; it's not for journalists to judge.

Label Acts, Not Groups

That said, journalists cannot, and should not, be blind to reality. When we see terrorism, we should say so. A suicide bombing on a crowded bus is clearly an act of terrorism and should be so labeled. And it should also be described in all its painful detail. Such reporting is more powerful in its specificity than any broad label.

This approach—call the act terrorist, but not the organization—is used in many news rooms, including the *Globe*'s. It allows for variations: The terrorist label can appear in a quote or when detailing Washington's official list of terrorist groups. But not in the reporter's own voice.

[It is best] to avoid attaching labels to either side, instead providing "accurate, fair and honest accounts of specific news events."

The wisdom of this approach is, understandably, the subject of renewed debate in the wake of [a] recent, horrible bus bombing in Jerusalem that killed 21 people. There are good arguments on both sides. But I cast my lot with those who believe the current approach—perhaps imperfect and a bit contrived—best serves accuracy and impartiality, at least for now. It is a necessary accommodation in a complicated world.

Describing Events vs. Labeling

"The overall approach here is to describe events and present facts rather than to attach labels to individuals or groups," notes *Globe* editor Martin Baron. "We particularly seek to avoid hot-button language that has become associated with a point of view. . . ."

Baron notes that Middle East coverage is a special concern for many readers. He acknowledges the view of supporters of Israel who "believe we should use the term 'terrorist' to describe militant Palestinian groups that encourage or carry out horrific suicide bombings against civilians"—and of Palestinians and their backers who "argue that theirs is a legitimate struggle over land and freedom . . . (and) that Israeli military killings of Palestinian civilians should be properly portrayed as 'state terrorism.'" The debate, he says, is complicated by the fact that some militant Palestinian groups also perform some social service functions.

Best, he says, to avoid attaching labels to either side, instead providing "accurate, fair and honest accounts of specific news events." That includes calling suicide bombings "acts of terror" and "terror attacks." (The *Globe* also routinely points out the State Department designation of Palestinian groups such as Hamas and Islamic Jihad as terrorist organizations.)

The *Globe* practice, says Baron, is to evaluate each story individually. In the "relatively rare" instances where the terrorism label is used broadly, he says, "it has been applied to groups that have no clearly identifiable or explicitly articulated political objective."

The Al Qaeda Exception

Count Al Qaeda as one of those exceptions. In the *Globe* and elsewhere, it's called a "terrorist network"—which prompts critics to argue, anew, that if Al Qaeda is a terrorist organization so is (fill the blank).

It's difficult, given that the definition of Al Qaeda in the United States is almost solely based on the 9/11 attacks, to imagine seeing it as anything else. A more precise definition—"a radical Islamist network that employs violence against innocents"—trumps "terrorist" on grounds of specificity, but it ignores one of our most profound national experiences, 9/11. Given Al Qaeda's self-definition and its large-scale embrace of terrorism, it has proven itself an allowable exception.

Media Decisions to Publish Graphic War Photographs Are Ethically Based

Kenny Irby

Kenny Irby is the visual journalism group leader and the director of diversity at the Poynter Institute, a not-for-profit organization dedicated to journalism education.

It is true that a picture can be worth 1,000 words. And it's also true that some pictures are worth 1,000 pictures. Especially in times of war, certain pictures have a unique way of changing the course of history.

Photos from Iraq . . . especially the images of prisoner abuse shown again and again . . . could be in that category: pictures that inform and influence the public in profound ways.

Tough Decisions

The decision to publish dramatic and tragic photographs that depict the horrors of war is never easy. Perhaps even the cave dwellers of ancient times felt unsettled as they drew detailed battle images on their walls. We do know that throughout the modern era of warfare and photography, journalists have struggled with achieving a balance between maximizing truthful reporting and minimizing unnecessary harm, and the graphic images from Iraq have ignited that struggle anew.

Newspapers across the country have made different decisions about whether to publish the new images that show abuse and even death, and they are likely to face more difficult decisions if new photographs and videotapes of even worse brutality become public. . . .

Yet by and large the U.S. media's principle is this: Citizens can make their own best choices when armed with honest information.

Iconic Photos

Consider the impact of certain iconic photos of past conflicts. There was the 1968 photo of South Vietnamese National Police Chief Brig. Gen. Nguyen Ngoc Loan executing a Viet Cong officer with a single pistol shot to the head in Saigon, as reported by Eddie Adams. There was also the photo of the napalm-seared 9-year-old Kim Phuc seeking help, documented in 1972 by Nick Ut.

More recently, recall the countless "Highway of Death" photographs from the 1991 Operation Desert Storm, especially one that showed an incinerated Iraqi soldier at the wheel of his vehicle. And lest we forget: a U.S. soldier's limp body being dragged through the dusty streets of Mogadishu, Somalia, by angry anti-American protesters, recorded in 1993 by Paul Watson.

Decisions about compelling and often disturbing photographs will never satisfy all of the people all of the time.

These photos earned journalistic recognition. Yet the greatest prize was informing the public on matters of world interest. All expanded public consciousness or in some way impacted policy: The Vietnam photos helped galvanize the anti-war effort and also encouraged other citizens to support the troops. The Somalia photo influenced President [Bill] Clinton's decision to withdraw troops from the African nation. The Highway of Death photos sullied the image of a quick, clean war.

The War in Iraq

Fast-forward to the war in Iraq. We've seen photos showing the murders of four contractors, the burning of their bodies, and the repugnant dismembering and hanging of torsos on a bridge in Al-Fallujah. And the photos of the melancholy garden of coffins draped in red, white, and blue in a plane's cargo area.

And the disgusting treatment of Iraqi prisoners of war by a few of America's soldiers. . . . The images of brutality have been broadcast and published around the world: Iraqi prisoners piled naked in a pyramid, a wired and hooded Iraqi, an inmate pinned under a stretcher, a female soldier holding a leash tied to the neck of a naked prisoner.

Such images are articles of visual information that convey messages of truth and report authentic facts in immeasurable ways. Journalists know that, citizens understand this, the American government tries to control this (the Pentagon acknowledged it had asked CBS to delay initial broadcasting of the prison images), and terrorists seek to abuse this.

Disturbing or Distasteful?

Thus, decisions about compelling and often disturbing photographs will never satisfy all of the people all of the time, and that is not the role of the messenger.

Newsroom leaders and decision-makers agonize over "doing the right thing" when trying to decide whether to show visual truths—and not just write about those truths—because the visual images are more searing.

"We are not taking a particular side" by publishing photos, said Michel duCille, picture editor of *The Washington Post*, after making the decision to publish prison photographs [in May 2004]. As Marcia Prouse, director of photography at the *Orange County Register* put it, "Does the news value of the photograph outweigh the taste factor?"

The Taste Test

How is "taste" defined? A dictionary definition might describe it as a form, style, or manner showing propriety. Newsrooms use less abstract tests, such as:

- How would a person react to this image over a bowl of Cheerios or a glass of orange juice?

- Does the photo show dead bodies?

- Does the photo show blood?

- Does the photo show people naked?

- What if my child saw this?

In many newsrooms around the country, some of the Iraq [prison] photos failed the litmus test. Many journalists argued against running the photos, just as many argued it was important to run them, but in the end certain images were not published. Indeed, many editors—reflecting the generally stricter litmus tests of the past 10-to-15 years—argue that viewers and readers don't want to see such pictures.

The primary role of photojournalism is to visually document and report on the significant events of the day.

On the other hand, some observers might say that newsroom leaders are too concerned with being besieged by calls, letters, and e-mails, or with facing subscription cancellations or channel changing.

Whatever their decision on the new photos, many news organizations disagree with the [George W.] Bush administration's ban on taking photos of dead soldiers' homecomings, a policy intended to show respect for the soldiers' families. "I believe there should be a free flow of information between the government and the media," said Jeff Cohen, editor of the *Houston Chronicle*.

Citizen Photojournalist

Complicating decisions these days are technological innovations and the ubiquitous digital cameras. Everywhere you look there are citizens with cameras challenging historic notions of who is a journalist.

In recent weeks we have seen a former Maytag Aircraft cargo worker—not a journalist—take photos of soldiers' coffins being loaded onto aircraft bound for the United States. She said she wanted to shed illumination on the care and integrity being rendered to America's fallen soldiers.

It was a citizen with a cause and a website—not a journalist—who filed a Freedom of Information Act request that led the Department of Defense to release several hundred photographs of dead soldiers' caskets arriving at Dover Air Force Base.

And it is ostensibly a U.S. soldier—not a journalist—who documented the interrogation tactics and objectionable actions in the Abu Ghurayb prison near Baghdad. Prouse of the *Orange County Register* notes that "there are fewer embedded photographers in the region and that the activities now are so spread out that the violence is more random," thus leading to more dependence for images on freelancers and civilians. She also is concerned that throughout this war there have been "a lot more images of the conflict" and thus the powerful iconic images are fewer and farther between.

Upsetting but Important

Whether it is with powerful still or video images, the primary role of photojournalism is to visually document and report on the significant events of the day and on the varied viewpoints in our common world.

As Americans sift through lots of images from Iraq, they ought to be able to trust that photographers and editors have thought enough about their choices to give them ones that, while they may be upsetting, will illuminate what they need to know about the impact of war on the people involved.

Media Decisions to Publish Stories That Could Harm National Security Are Ethically Based

Dean Baquet and Bill Keller

Dean Baquet was editor of the Los Angeles Times *when this viewpoint was written and now heads the Washington, D.C., bureau of the* New York Times. *Bill Keller is the executive editor of the* New York Times.

Since Sept. 11, 2001, newspaper editors have faced excruciating choices in covering the government's efforts to protect the country from terrorist agents. Each of us has, on a number of occasions, withheld information because we were convinced that publishing it could put lives at risk. On other occasions, each of us has decided to publish classified information over strong objections from our government.

[On June 23, 2006, the *New York Times* and *Los Angeles Times*] disclosed a secret [George W.] Bush administration program to monitor international banking transactions. We did so after appeals from senior administration officials to hold the story. Our reports—like earlier press disclosures of secret measures to combat terrorism—revived an emotional national debate, featuring angry calls of "treason" and proposals that journalists be jailed along with much genuine concern and confusion about the role of the press in times like these.

The Responsibilities of the Press

We are rivals. Our newspapers compete on a hundred fronts every day. We apply the principles of journalism individually as editors of independent newspapers. We agree, however, on some basics about the immense responsibility the press has been given by the inventors of the country.

Make no mistake, journalists have a large and personal stake in the country's security. We live and work in cities that have been tragically marked as terrorist targets. Reporters and photographers from both our papers braved the collapsing towers to convey the horror to the world.

We have correspondents today alongside troops on the front lines in Iraq and Afghanistan. Others risk their lives in a quest to understand the terrorist threat; Daniel Pearl of *The Wall Street Journal* was murdered on such a mission. We, and the people who work for us, are not neutral in the struggle against terrorism.

The conflict between the government's passion for secrecy and the press's drive to reveal is not of recent origin.

But the virulent hatred espoused by terrorists, judging by their literature, is directed not just against our people and our buildings. It is also aimed at our values, at our freedoms and at our faith in the self-government of an informed electorate. If the freedom of the press makes some Americans uneasy, it is anathema to the ideologists of terror.

The Government vs. the Press

[On June 30, 1971], in the Supreme Court ruling that stopped the government from suppressing the secret Vietnam War history called the Pentagon Papers, Justice Hugo Black wrote: "The government's power to censor the press was abolished so that the press would remain forever free to censure the government. The press was protected so that it could bare the secrets of the government and inform the people."

As that sliver of judicial history reminds us, the conflict between the government's passion for secrecy and the press's drive to reveal is not of recent origin. This did not begin with the Bush administration, although the polarization of the electorate and the daunting challenge of terrorism have made the tension between press and government as clamorous as at any time since Justice Black wrote.

Our job, especially in times like these, is to bring our readers information that will enable them to judge how well their elected leaders are fighting on their behalf, and at what price.

In recent years our papers have brought you a great deal of information the White House never intended for you to know—classified secrets about the questionable intelligence that led the country to war in Iraq, about the abuse of prisoners in Iraq and Afghanistan, about the transfer of suspects to countries that are not squeamish about using torture, about eavesdropping without warrants.

As Robert G. Kaiser, associate editor of *The Washington Post*, asked recently in the pages of that newspaper: "You may have been shocked by these revelations, or not at all disturbed by them, but would you have preferred not to know them at all? If a war is being waged in America's name, shouldn't Americans understand how it is being waged?"

How do we, as editors, reconcile the obligation to inform with the instinct to protect?

Government officials, understandably, want it both ways. They want us to protect their secrets, and they want us to trumpet their successes. Treasury Secretary John Snow said he was scandalized by our decision to report on the bank-monitoring program. But in September 2003 the same Secretary Snow invited a group of reporters from our papers, *The Wall Street Journal* and others to travel with him and his aides on a military aircraft for a six-day tour to show off the department's efforts to track terrorist financing. The secretary's team discussed many sensitive details of their monitoring efforts, hoping they would appear in print and demonstrate the administration's relentlessness against the terrorist threat.

Inform, or Protect?

How do we, as editors, reconcile the obligation to inform with the instinct to protect?

Sometimes the judgments are easy. Our reporters in Iraq and Afghanistan, for example, take great care not to divulge operational intelligence in their news reports, knowing that in this wired age it could be seen and used by insurgents.

Often the judgments are painfully hard. In those cases, we cool our competitive jets and begin an intensive deliberative process.

The process begins with reporting. Sensitive stories do not fall into our hands. They may begin with a tip from a source who has a grievance or a guilty conscience, but those tips are just the beginning of long, painstaking work. Reporters operate without security clearances, without subpoena powers, without spy technology. They work, rather, with sources who may be scared, who may know only part of the story, who may have their own agendas that need to be discovered and taken into account. We double-check and triple-check. We seek out sources with different points of view. We challenge our sources when contradictory information emerges.

Then we listen. No article on a classified program gets published until the responsible officials have been given a fair opportunity to comment. And if they want to argue that publication represents a danger to national security, we put things on hold and give them a respectful hearing. Often, we agree to participate in off-the-record conversations with officials, so they can make their case without fear of spilling more secrets onto our front pages.

Finally, we weigh the merits of publishing against the risks of publishing. There is no magic formula, no neat metric for either the public's interest or the dangers of publishing sensitive information. We make our best judgment.

Deciding to Withhold

When we come down in favor of publishing, of course, everyone hears about it. Few people are aware when we decide to hold an article. But each of us, in the past few years, has had the experience of withholding or delaying articles when the administration convinced us that the risk of publication outweighed the benefits. Probably the most discussed instance was *The New York Times*'s decision to hold its article on telephone eavesdropping for more than a year, until editors felt that further reporting had whittled away the administration's case for secrecy.

But there are other examples. *The New York Times* has held articles that, if published, might have jeopardized efforts to protect vulnerable stockpiles of nuclear material, and articles about highly sensitive counterterrorism initiatives that are still in operation. *The Los Angeles Times* withheld information about American espionage and surveillance activities in Afghanistan discovered on computer drives purchased by reporters in an Afghan bazaar.

It is not always a matter of publishing an article or killing it. Sometimes we deal with the security concerns by editing out gratuitous detail that lends little to public understanding but might be useful to the targets of surveillance. *The Washington Post*, at the administration's request, agreed not to name the specific countries that had secret Central Intelligence Agency prisons, deeming that information not essential for American readers. *The New York Times*, in its article on National Security Agency eavesdropping, left out some technical details.

Even the banking articles, which the president and vice president have condemned, did not dwell on the operational or technical aspects of the program, but on its sweep, the questions about its legal basis and the issues of oversight.

An Editorial Responsibility

We understand that honorable people may disagree with any of these choices—to publish or not to publish. But making those decisions is the responsibility that falls to editors, a corollary to the great gift of our independence. It is not a responsibility we take lightly. And it is not one we can surrender to the government.

The Media Should Call People Who Attack Civilians "Terrorists"

Andrea Levin

Andrea Levin is the executive director of the Committee for Accuracy in Middle East Reporting in America (CAMERA), a not-for-profit organization that fights anti-Israel bias in the media.

The intense controversy surrounding the reluctance of Reuters and other media outlets to use the word "terrorist" says a lot about how abhorrent are the deeds of those branded with the term. Terrorists themselves typically shun the label, preferring euphemisms that disguise their actions.

Taking Sides

Why do media outlets follow suit? Some reporters and editors fear that the use of accurate terminology will compromise sources close to terrorist organizations, or even make the media organizations a target for retribution. A travel advisory for journalists in Gaza by Reuters' Nidal al-Mughrabi cautions colleagues to "never use the word terrorist or terrorism in describing Palestinian gunmen and militants" lest offence be given.

The more commonly traded explanation for using vague words such as "militant" and "activist" to describe terrorists is a supposedly high-minded adherence to professional neutrality. Reuters and others claim to be eschewing "emotive" or partisan language, instead confining coverage to specific, detailed descriptions of events and perpetrators.

But avoiding use of the word "terrorist" is actually imprecise and misleading. It is tantamount to taking sides—the terrorist's side.

Terrorism in Beslan

The seizure, for instance, of more than 1,000 civilians in Beslan [Russia], many of them children, and their brutal incarceration for days without food and water, and then the slaughter of hundreds in an inferno of bombs and shooting, is not merely the work of "gunmen," "militants," "guerillas" or "insurgents." While these might be the preferred, sanitized terms of the killers themselves, they do not accurately convey either the ghastly episode or the intent of the perpetrators.

Terrorizing a population through displays of extreme cruelty against non-combatants to achieve political gains was the aim of the hostage-takers. That is terrorism.

Terrorism in Beslan, like that inflicted in Bali or New York or Spain or Morocco, is a phenomenon that conforms to a very specific definition. To suggest the atrocities committed and those who perform them should not be identified for what they are denies readers and viewers essential information about the forces that shape the world in which we live.

Palestinian Terrorism

But nowhere are the verbal gyrations and inconsistencies on the subject more apparent than in the heavily reported arena of the Arab-Israeli conflict. Here, many media follow a relentless policy of interjecting softened synonyms for "terrorist."

For instance, a Reuters story from June 6, 2004, reported on the sentencing of Palestinian leader Marwan Barghouti, convicted of terrorist activity by Israeli courts. The article stated that he "denied involvement in militant ambushes," and noted that he was given a 20-year prison term for participating in a "terror group"—with scare quotes making clear this was Israel's term, not Reuters'.

The "militant ambush" referred to so briefly in the piece, in fact, entailed the terrorist killing of a Greek Orthodox monk with a bullet through the neck while he drove in a vehicle bearing Israeli licence plates. Other crimes by "militants" in which "revolt leader" Barghouti was implicated include the March 5, 2002, killings of three people in a Tel Aviv restaurant. A member of the al-Aqsa Martyrs Brigade sprayed gunfire into the street, threw grenades into a restaurant and then—once his ammunition ran out—began stabbing passersby with a knife. In addition to the dead, 30 were wounded.

Newspapers have a duty to their readers to give preference to truth over obfuscation.

The Barghouti piece is notable since it involves a man lauded by Palestinians and now tried and convicted by Israel. The language of the news report skews toward the word preferences of Barghouti and his followers, and against Israel. For Reuters' clients, including the *National Post*, correcting such language is simply a matter of good journalism.

Misleading Language

In their efforts to circumvent reference to the "T-word" altogether, media outlets sometimes misrepresent quotes and statements from public figures. On April 20, 2004, for instance, a dispatch by [Reuters] led with: "Prime Minister Ariel Sharon pledged on Tuesday Israel would keep killing Palestinian militants after the assassination of two top Hamas leaders."

Sharon did not, of course, pledge to continue hunting down "militants"; he said "we will fight terror and we will not let up on them." In muting the language, Reuters also changes the sense of the report to a degree. After all, an ongoing policy of "killing" terrorists is patently justifiable, while one devoted to "killing Palestinian militants" conjures up something different.

If Reuters, or any other wire service, routinely substitutes gentler, inexact language for statements such as these and for deeds manifestly those of a terrorist, by what logic should a newspaper using the agency's copy not edit back into stories more accurate language?

Wire services may feel the sanitized language helps their reporters in the field ingratiate themselves with the violent groups they are covering. But newspapers have a duty to their readers to give preference to truth over obfuscation.

The Media Should Report More Often on the Heroism of American Soldiers

Jeff Emanuel

Jeff Emanuel is former director of RedState.com, a popular conservative blog; a special operations veteran of the Iraq war; a fellow at the University of Georgia's Center for International Trade and Security; and a Pulitzer Prize–nominated combat journalist whose writings can be seen at www.jeffemanuel.net.

Last November 1 [2007], *The American Spectator* [*TAS*] published an exclusive account of four American paratroopers who'd fought to thwart a massive al Qaeda kidnap-and-execution operation in the Iraqi city of Samarra.

Caught completely by surprise and outnumbered at least ten to one by heavily-armed fighters, the four young soldiers—Sergeant Josh Morley, Specialist Tracy Willis, and then-Specialists Eric Moser and Chris Corriveau—fought a pitched and protracted rooftop battle that left at least a dozen terrorists dead, and made the surviving Americans into heroes.

Sergeant Morley and Specialist Willis lost their lives in the encounter. Morley left behind an infant daughter he had never met.

Recognizing "Our" Heroes

After *TAS* broke the story, it faded out of the news for nearly seven months, with the only media mention of the harrowing event coming in an editorial by William Kristol and Dean Barnett in the *Weekly Standard*, which contrasted the bravery of these soldiers with the attitude of American diplomats who were making news at the time by very publicly refusing assignments to Baghdad.

The story of that rooftop battle came to life once again when, on May 22, 2008, now-Sergeants Moser and Corriveau were presented with Distinguished Service Crosses by President George W. Bush for their heroism and gallantry under fire on that fateful morning half a world away. (A compilation of photographs and video interviews is available [at http://jeffemanuel.net/bittersweet-honors-for-heroes-of-samarra-ambush]).

According to the U.S. Army Institute of Heraldry, the Distinguished Service Cross, which is second only to the Medal of Honor in the hierarchy of decorations, "is awarded to a person who while serving in any capacity with the Army, distinguished himself or herself by extraordinary heroism ... while engaged in an action against an enemy of the United States."

The recognition these paratroopers have received is well deserved ... these young men are entirely deserving of the highest award that their country can possibly offer them: the Medal of Honor.

"*The act or acts of heroism must have been so notable and have involved risk of life so extraordinary as to set the individual apart from his or her comrades*" (emphasis added).

Ordinary Men

As is obvious to all who have read or heard of their amazing story, the actions of Eric Moser and Chris Corriveau fit that description almost to a "T." As the military hierarchy from President Bush down has recognized, Sergeants Moser and Corriveau are heroes in every sense of the word—not that you would get that impression from talking to them.

Both Eric Moser and Chris Corriveau are ordinary young men who, when the literal fight of their lives broke out with no warning whatsoever, reacted with such extraordinary focus, resolve, and reflexive action that they not only held off an overwhelmingly larger enemy force and managed to save their own lives in the process, but also succeeded in protecting the bodies of their fallen comrades from concerted efforts made by the attackers to claim at least one of those American soldiers' bodies as a prize.

The recognition these paratroopers have received is well deserved—though in my personal opinion, as a veteran and as the reporter who repeatedly interviewed all participants and went over the situation that they faced, in the place that they faced it, so as better to understand those events before the authoring the story for *TAS*, these young men are entirely deserving of the highest award that their country can possibly offer them: the Medal of Honor.

Recognition, though, does not take away the scarring effects of that battle, nor does it bring back from the dead those who were lost. In an interview with CBS News after President Bush presented him with his award, Corriveau honestly downplayed his own actions and their effects—saying that, truly, "I almost wanted to die that day on the roof with my brothers."

A Story Worth Covering

With the President's attendance at the 82nd Airborne Division's "All-American Week" events, and his presentation of these awards to Sergeants Moser and Corriveau, the mainstream media has decided that their story is not only believable, but actually worth covering. However, as with all acts of bravery, and all actions that put something greater above one's self, neither recognition nor media attention is necessary to validate these young men's actions, nor to confirm that they are indeed heroes.

Having completed a fifteen-month combat tour in Iraq and returned to the United States in November [2007], the 82nd Airborne is reportedly scheduled to deploy back to the Middle East this fall [2008]. When it does so, it will be short at least four soldiers.

New Beginnings

Chris Corriveau, still scarred by the events that robbed him of his two best friends in the world, has said he plans to separate from the Army and attend college this fall.

Eric Moser attended the Special Forces Assessment and Selection course and was selected to begin Special Forces training. In the fall, he takes his first steps toward trading in the maroon beret of a paratrooper that he currently wears for the Green Beret of an Army Special Forces soldier.

Josh Morley and Tracy Willis, who lost their lives during that fateful gun battle in Samarra (and who were posthumously awarded Bronze Star Medals for their actions), will always be cherished and remembered by those who knew them, as well as by those millions of Americans who value the risks and sacrifices our military men and women make in the name of their comrades and of our freedoms, often at the highest possible cost.

The Media Should Publish Graphic Photographs of the War in Iraq

Gary Kamiya

Gary Kamiya is a writer at large for Salon.com, an online news and commentary magazine.

This is a war the [George W.] Bush administration does not want Americans to see. From the beginning, the U.S. government has attempted to censor information about the Iraq war, prohibiting photographs of the coffins of U.S. troops returning home and refusing as a matter of policy to keep track of the number of Iraqis who have been killed. President Bush has yet to attend a single funeral of a soldier killed in Iraq.

Powerful Images

To be sure, this see-no-evil approach is neither surprising nor new. With the qualified exception of the Vietnam War, when images of body bags appeared frequently on the nightly news, American governments have always tightly controlled images of war. There is good reason for this. In war, a picture really is worth a thousand words. No story about a battle, no matter how eloquent, possesses the raw power of a photograph. And when it comes to war's ultimate consequences—death and suffering—there is simply no comparison: a photo of a dead man or woman has the capacity to unsettle those who see it, sometimes forever. The bloated corpses photographed by Mathew Brady after [the Civil War battle of] Antietam remain in the mind, their puffy, shocked faces haunting us like an obscene truth almost 150 years after the soldiers were cut down.

Gary Kamiya, "Iraq: The Unseen War," Salon.com, August 23, 2005. This article first appeared in Salon.com, at http://www.salon.com. An online version remains in the Salon archives. Reprinted with permission.

"War is hell," said Gen. [William T.] Sherman, and everyone dutifully agrees. Yet the hell in Iraq is almost never shown. The few exceptions—the charred bodies of American contractors hanging from a bridge in Fallujah, the blood-spattered little girl wailing after her parents were killed next to her—only prove the rule.

Governments keep war hidden because it is hideous. To allow citizens to see its reality—the shattered bodies, the wounded children, the incomprehensible mayhem—is to risk eroding popular support for it. This is particularly true with wars that have less than overwhelming popular support to begin with. In the case of Vietnam, battlefield images played an important role in turning the tide of public opinion. And in Iraq, a war whose official justification has turned out to be false, and which a majority of the American people now believe to have been a mistake, the administration would prefer that these grim images never be seen.

Media Reluctance

But the media is also responsible for sanitizing the Iraq war, at times rendering it almost invisible. Most American publications have been reluctant to run graphic war images. Almost no photographs of the 1,868 U.S. troops who have been killed [as of August 2005] in Iraq have appeared in U.S. publications. In May 2005, the *Los Angeles Times* surveyed six major newspapers and the nation's two leading newsmagazines, and found that over a six-month period, no images of dead American troops appeared in the *New York Times, Washington Post, Los Angeles Times, St. Louis Post-Dispatch, Atlanta Journal-Constitution, Time* or *Newsweek*. A single image of a covered body of a slain American ran in the *Seattle Times*. There were also comparatively few images of wounded Americans. The publications surveyed tended to run more images of dead or wounded Iraqis, but they have hardly been depicted in large numbers either.

There are a number of reasons why the media has shied away from running graphic images from Iraq. Some are simple logistics: There are very few photographers in Iraq. Freelance reporter and photographer Mitchell Prothero, a *Salon* contributor, estimates there are "maybe a dozen or two Western photographers" in Iraq, in addition to Iraqi and Arab stringers, who do most of the work for newswires. Ten or 20 photographers trying to cover a country the size of Sweden, under extremely difficult and dangerous conditions, are unlikely to be on the scene when violence erupts.

Relations with the Military

Moreover, most photographers are embedded with U.S. troops, a situation that imposes its own limits. Military regulations prevent photographers from publishing photographs of dead or wounded soldiers until their families have been notified, which can diminish the news value of the photographs. And although embed rules allow photographers to take pictures of dead or wounded troops, the reality on the ground can be different. Soldiers do not want photographers—especially ones they aren't comfortable with—taking pictures of their dead or wounded buddies. This is understandable, but it can result in de facto censorship.

One photographer, who requested anonymity because he didn't want to jeopardize his ongoing relationship with the U.S. military, told *Salon*, "I've had unit commanders tell me flat out that if anybody gets wounded on patrol, you can't take any pictures of them. Nearly every time I've landed at [a medevac] scene, guys have yelled at me, 'Get the f--- away from me. Don't take my friend's picture. Get back on the helicopter.' Part of me understands that. I am a stranger to them. And they are very emotional. Their friend has been badly hurt or wounded, and they've probably all just been shot at 15 minutes before. I totally understand that, although it is a violation of embed rules."

Cautious Editors

But it isn't just the troops. Editors in the States are reluctant to run graphic photographs. There are various reasons for this. Perhaps the most important is taste: Many publications think graphic images are just too disturbing. Business considerations doubtless also play a role, although few editors would admit that; graphic images upset some readers and can scare off advertisers. . . . And there are political considerations: Supporters of the war often accuse the media of playing up bad news at the expense of more positive developments. To run images of corpses is to risk being criticized of antiwar bias. When "Nightline" ran photographs of the faces of all the U.S. troops who had been killed in Iraq, conservative groups were enraged and accused the network of harming morale. Not every publisher is anxious to walk into this kind of trouble.

The reluctance of American publications to run shocking images contrasts with the European press. "In my experience and in conversations with other people who've been doing this a lot longer than me, American publications shy away from extremely graphic material, compared to European ones," says Prothero. "I don't know whether the American audience reacts more strongly against seeing that over the breakfast table. I do know, anecdotally, that many very talented photographers, on staff, have taken pictures that have not run in magazines or newspapers. Maybe it's not a conscious decision but American publications very much shy away from showing casualties of U.S. troops on the ground. I think they're afraid the American public will freak out on them for showing dead American boys."

A Photo of a Dead Girl

Photographer Stephanie Sinclair's unforgettable photograph of a 6-year-old Iraqi girl killed by an American cluster bomb . . . originally ran in the *Chicago Tribune*. Robin Daughtridge, the *Tribune*'s deputy director of photography, told *Salon* that after the photographs first came in, "the news editor was worried about running them without an accompanying story." Others in the newsroom thought the photographs "were too graphic, and too much, because we generally don't run tight pictures of dead bodies. We had run pictures of dead Iraqi soldiers and a dead bus driver before, so there was a precedent for running them, but we don't take it lightly." They ended up calling the paper's editor in chief, Ann Marie Lipinski, who assigned a reporter to do a piece on cluster bombs and their legacy.

Ultimately, Daughtridge, said, politics didn't enter into the decision: "It was more about the fact that if we're going to show this death up close and personal, we better have a story behind it. All of us in the newsroom are trying to tell the story and letting the readers make up their own minds." She added, "I felt proud of what we did that day. All of this stuff that you hear about happening to families in Iraq doesn't really hit home until you see that picture of the little girl."

For her part, Sinclair praised the *Tribune* for running the photo and the story. But, she said, "some of the publications I've worked for didn't run a lot of the Iraqi civilian stuff, the graphic pictures, the emotional pictures. I found that the Iraqi civilian story was really hard to get published in U.S. publications. And I worked for many. I don't know why. I think they're looking at their readership and they think their readers want to know about American troops, since they can relate to them more. They think that's what the audience wants."

People should know the truth about war.

Sinclair also noted that American readers and viewers get only a sanitized view of the horrific consequences of suicide bombings. "A lot of the bombing stuff that you see is really toned down. To be honest, sometimes it should be. God, it's relentless. It's hard to look at. People have no idea what's happening in Iraq. You wonder, even as a photographer, if you're being gratuitous by photographing some of this. At the same time, as horrific as it is to see, people should know how horrific it is to live it every day. We should feel some sort of responsibility to make sure we have the best possible grasp of what's happening there."

The Truth Should Be Told

It is because we believe that the American people are not getting a look at the reality of the Iraq war, for Americans and Iraqis alike, that we decided to run this photo gallery [accompanying the online story]. It is no secret that *Salon* has published many more pieces questioning and challenging the Iraq war than supporting it. But that is not why we think it is important that these images be seen. We would have run them even if we supported the war. The reason is simple: The truth should be told. People should know the truth about war. Before a nation decides to go to war, it should know what its consequences are.

There is no way for any journalist, whether reporter or photographer, to capture the multifaceted reality of Iraq. But all of the journalists I have spoken to who have worked in Iraq say that the blandly optimistic pronouncements made by the Bush administration about the situation in Iraq are completely false. A picture of a dead child only represents a fragment of the truth about Iraq—but it is one that we do not have the right to ignore. We believe we have an ethical responsibility to those who have been killed or wounded, whether Iraqis, Americans or those of other nationalities, not to simply pretend that their fate never happened. To face the bitter truth of war is painful. But it is better than hiding one's eyes.

CHAPTER 4

When Should Journalists Abandon Neutrality?

Chapter Preface

One of the major ethical values of modern journalism is neutrality: the idea that journalists should not favor one side or point of view over another in a conflict. Instead, media ethicists say, journalists should report the facts and the arguments of each side evenhandedly and allow readers and viewers to draw their own conclusions.

The belief that the media ought to be neutral is deeply entrenched in the United States, not just among journalists but also among the people who read and watch the news. Even though polls show that a majority of Americans believe that the media *is* biased, almost no one thinks that the media *should be* biased. The Fox News Channel, which is widely viewed as the conservative alternative to the supposedly liberally biased CNN, bills itself not as "the news channel for conservatives" but as the "fair and balanced" news channel. There are a number of media watchdog groups, on the political left and the right, which exist to document alleged bias in the media. These groups typically claim that their goal is to eliminate bias in the news, not to make sure that the news is biased in their direction, even though they usually focus only on pointing out media bias against their own political views. The fact that organizations such as these feel the need to portray themselves as advocating for or carrying out fair and accurate reporting, rather than reporting that is more favorable to their and their audience's political positions, shows just how deeply the value of journalistic neutrality is held.

However, despite the seemingly universal consensus around the idea that journalism should be neutral and objective, this idea is relatively new. In the eighteenth and nineteenth centuries American newspapers were highly partisan, making no secret of the fact that they reported the news from a specific political perspective, and newspaper owners and reporters did not shy away from becoming involved in politics themselves. Joseph Pulitzer, one of the men who is credited with creating modern newspaper journalism and for whom journalism's highest award is named, briefly served in the U.S. Congress while continuing to run the *St. Louis Post-Dispatch*. As late as 1920 both the Republicans and the Democrats nominated the owners of partisan newspapers as their presidential candidates: Warren G. Harding for the Republicans and James M. Cox for the Democrats.

Although a consensus that the media should be neutral developed in the United States during the twentieth century, the importance of journalistic neutrality is still contested by many outside the American journalistic mainstream. In Europe, for example, the partisan press thrived long after it had died out in the United States. Even today some European countries have newspapers that are openly affiliated with a political party. Few people in the United States are advocating a return to the days of party-affiliated newspapers, but some journalists have begun to question whether there is now too much emphasis on the media being completely neutral and objective. The authors in the following chapter debate when—if ever—modern-day journalists might need to abandon their neutrality to do their jobs effectively and ethically.

The Media Should Emphasize Fact over Opinion

Joe Saltzman

Joe Saltzman is associate mass media editor of USA Today *maga-zine, associate dean and professor of journalism at the University of Southern California's Annenberg School of Communication in Los Angeles, director of the Norman Lear Center project Image of the Journalist in Popular Culture, and the author of* Frank Ca-pra and the Image of the Journalist in American Film.

Some commentators call it "faux news;" others refer to it as "fake news." It is not just "The Daily Show with Jon Stew-art" and "The Colbert Report with Steven Colbert"—cited as the primary news sources for millions of people. It is the mainstream news media blowing up minor, unimportant events into "fake news" that replaces "real news" about impor-tant subjects. This affliction can influence any type of story and is the bread-and-butter of celebrity news. However, it par-ticularly is annoying when it takes over serious news stories in areas that dramatically affect our lives, including politics, eco-nomics, and science.

For example, the overwhelming and continuous coverage of the misstatement by Sen. John Kerry (D.-Mass.) concerning soldiers in Iraq swamped all other political coverage about is-sues or candidates in the November 2006 elections. All Kerry did was leave out a two-letter word, "us." The Republicans, looking for anything to distance themselves from the disas-trous war in Iraq and ever-growing budget deficit, claimed Kerry was dissing the loyal troops fighting our war. Then the news media rushed in for the kill. Kerry's attack on [George W.] Bush's handling of the war was lost in the error—"Do you know where you end up if you don't study, if you aren't smart, if you're intellectually lazy? You end up getting [us] stuck in a war in Iraq. Just ask President Bush." Reporters, commentators, and comics joined the Republicans in hazing the former Democratic candidate for president. The news media picked up the story attributed to "White House and Republican allies" and it dominated the headlines and TV newscasts for several days leading up to the elections. It replaced serious news coverage by emphasizing one minor gaffe. Even seasoned political reporters jumped on the bandwagon by writing stories analyzing the way the media covered the event, thus giving more publicity to the nonstory. It serves as one important example of a false news event given the status of real news in political coverage.

Taking the Easy Way Out

Pres. George Bush's miscues in grammar and relating facts usually take precedence over his far more serious errors in foreign policy and domestic economics. Mispronounced names and syntax slips become an uncomplicated story good for an easy laugh. Holding the President and his Cabinet responsible for a botched war effort or the largest deficit in this country's history is more difficult to report and write about. Real news always is.

In false news, credentials and experience simply do not matter.

Instead of presenting the issues of both sides of important political and economic issues, reporters treat elections and the economy as sporting events or horse races—who is the favorite and what are his or her odds of winning, and by how much? What stocks are front-runners? How high did the stock market go today?

Covering politics or the economy becomes a numbers game, with the news media reduced to being second-rate handicappers trying to predict the outcome. These amateur prognosticators are abetted by one meaningless poll after another. No one seems to care that many of these polls are run by special interests, usually Republicans [GOP] or Democrats. GOP internal polls usually say the Republican candidate is going to win or is doing better than expected. Democratic internal polls say the Democratic candidate is going to win or is doing better than expected. The news media print both polls as if they were valid indicators of what is going to happen on Election Day. How these polls were taken, the methodology used, the actual sampling amount—this information seldom is included in the story. The false story is: Who is going to win and by how much. Little attention is paid to what each candidate stands for or the issues involved. The real news is ignored in favor of reporting a horse race.

False News Kills Good Reporting

False news destroys good science reporting. The scientific reasoning behind global warming is reduced to a boxing match in which two sides duke it out with platitudes and insults. Those with no scientific background who merely have a set of beliefs to back up their opinions are given equal time with individuals who have spent a lifetime studying a particular phenomenon. Facts are ignored in place of opinion. All voices are given equal time and equal value by the press. In false news, credentials and experience simply do not matter. It is personality and celebrity status that dominate. How you say something becomes more important than what you say. It is style over substance. In the world of fake news, the punch line is everything. If what you say is funny or clever enough, it really does not matter if it is based on fact or superstition. Fake news will crown you the winner of any debate if you are clever enough to win it. Pity the poor scientist, economist, or politician who does not understand this; they usually end up being ridiculed and slandered. Experts become alarmists. War heroes become cowards. Patriots become traitors. Democrats become liberals. Republicans become right-wing fanatics. Welcome to the wonderful world of fake news.

Giving the country a diet of one-liners and simple stories based on irrelevant events makes it more difficult for serious reporters to offer a responsible digest of the day's news. Who likes bad news? Who doesn't want a quick laugh at somebody else's expense? Having two public personalities fight each other on the airwaves and in print is far more popular than reading a comprehensive report on global warming, embryonic stem cell research, or a key issue in an election.

Fake news lets everyone off the hook by creating a world in which we can laugh off anything no matter how serious or important it turns out to be. It's a world where lessons of the past are ignored, expertise is ridiculed, and the one who laughs last laughs best. Welcome to Armageddon Life.

Opinionated Journalism Is Good for Democracy

Victor Navasky

Victor Navasky is the former publisher and editorial director of the Nation, *an American opinion journal. He is also a professor at the Columbia University School of Journalism.*

It used to be that taking potshots at the media was a right-left thing. From [Spiro] Agnew/[William] Safire we got "nattering nabobs of negativism," and from [Noam] Chomsky/[Edward] Herman we got a "propaganda model" manufacturing mass consent. On the right, Accuracy in Media and on the left, Fairness & Accuracy in Reporting.

These days it's a little more complicated: The right complains about the liberal media (and Eric Alterman denies it even exists in his book "What Liberal Media?"). The left charges that it lacks media access, and "fair and balanced" Bill O'Reilly invites "these pinheads" (me included) to come on his [Fox News] program and be insulted and interrupted by him.

A New Complaint

Now something new has been added. The problem is not left- or right-wing journalism; It's not even journalism that's "top to bottom," (as populist Jim Hightower puts it). It's opinion journalism, period.

David Westin, the president of ABC News, told students at Harvard's Kennedy School [of Government]: "There's too much opinion journalism and not enough objective journalism." Or read the august Committee of Concerned Journalists complaining in its noble statement of purpose that "serious journalistic organizations drift toward opinion, entertainment and sensation"—making opinion guilty by association.

I have no brief for or against bloggers, and I can take or leave shout shows. But to me the problem is not too much opinion, it's too little. That's because the journalists I have most admired—including I.F. Stone, a Jeffersonian Marxist; Carey McWilliams, the rebel-radical, Lincoln Stefens, crusading investigator; Mary McGrory, bleeding-heart liberal (to speak only of the dead)—were all opinion journalists. I joined the cause when I took over at the opinionated *Nation* in 1978.

History of Opinion Journals

A few years ago, I set out to write a history of the journal of opinion, of magazines like *the Nation* and the *National Review*, which, as the latter's editor remarked, "exist to make a point, not a profit." As far as I knew, nobody had written such a book. That shows how much I knew.

It turned out that in 1962 Jurgen Habermas, the Frankfurt School philosopher, had published a definitive history of opinion journals. I hadn't heard of it—possibly because it was not translated into English until 1989, when it appeared under the catchy title "The Structural Transformation of the Public Sphere: An Inquiry into a Category of Bourgeois Society."

The information that democracy requires can be generated not by 'the facts' but only by . . . rigorous and vigorous policy debate.

Habermas' theory of the public sphere, in the Enlightenment tradition, is based on the idea that to flourish, democracy requires open argumentation and debate. This happened (at least for white males) in the city-states of ancient Greece and again in Europe, where, by the 18th century, public argument and debate flourished in coffeehouses and taverns.

Habermas organically linked the public sphere—a category halfway between government and the private or personal sphere—to the opinion journal. Coffeehouses (there were 3,000 in London alone) began to publish newsletters reporting on princes, noblemen and the court. They ended by criticizing those they covered, and they set the agenda for public debate.

The Role of Journalism

It all made such sense to me that I journeyed to Frankfurt, where I got the chance to ask him what I thought was the $64,000 question: What is—what should be—the role of the journal of opinion in the modern era? His answer may seem to be a platitude, but to me it had all the clarity of the Liberty Bell. "At the core of their mission," he said, "is to maintain the discursive character of public communication. Who else if not this type of press is going to set the standards?"

To set the standard for public discourse. Not bad.

Asking the Right Questions

[In March 2005], Westin followed up his anti-opinion speech at Harvard with an article in the *Columbia Journalism Review*: "The more we fill up our reports with opinion," he wrote, "the less time we have for reporting the facts."

But suppose the purpose of opinion journalism is less to develop the facts (unless they are missing from the mass media) than to ask the right questions? Suppose the information that democracy requires can be generated not by "the facts" but only by the rigorous and vigorous policy debate and moral argument that journals of opinion were founded to provide? Suppose, as the historian Christopher Lasch, who regretted our lapse into what he called a spectator society, was right when he observed that "information, usually seen as the pre-condition of debate, is better seen as the by-product"?

The fact is that shout shows or no shout shows, blogs or no blogs, like [comedian] Rodney Dangerfield, opinion journalism deserves a little respect.

Journalistic Independence Is More Important than Neutrality

Robert Jensen

Robert Jensen teaches journalism at the University of Texas at Austin.

In a recent discussion with other journalism professors, I suggested that mainstream journalists have failed to grasp the depth of the crises—cultural and political, economic and ecological—that the United States and modern industrial society face, and hence are failing in their fundamental task in a democratic society, the work of monitoring the centers of power.

A colleague acknowledged the importance of such issues, but said that university schools of journalism don't teach "advocacy journalism" or promote the idea of "the journalist as activist."

Propaganda and Advocacy

This advocacy/activist tag is often applied to journalists who don't accept the conventional wisdom of the powerful and dare to challenge the more basic frameworks within which news is reported. The idea seems to be that anyone who doesn't fall in line with the worldview of the powerful people and institutions in society is not "objective," and therefore must be motivated not by a principled search for truth but some pre-determined political agenda.

But the crucial distinction is not between "objective" and "advocacy/activist" journalists but (1) between propagandists and journalists, and then (2) between journalists who do the

Robert Jensen, "Beyond Advocacy v. Objective Journalism," *Znet*, July 28, 2007. Reproduced by permission of the author.

job well and those who do it poorly. If there is a label we might valorize, it should be "independent"—we need journalists who are independent not only from the powerful but also from any political movements.

While this may seem to be a hyper-sensitivity about terminology, an examination of these labels can help us understand both the problems with, and possibilities of, contemporary journalism.

The term *advocacy journalism* typically is used to describe the use of techniques to promote a specific political or social cause. The term is potentially meaningful only in opposition to a category of journalism that does not engage in advocacy, so-called *objective* journalism.

The Partisan Press

This distinction is a focus of attention most intensely in the United States, especially in the last half of the 20th century; use of these terms does not necessarily translate for other political landscapes, though U.S. (and more generally Western) models are becoming dominant. In Western Europe, some newspapers have long identified openly with a political position, even though journalists from those papers are considered professionals not typically engaged in advocacy. For example, in Italy *Il Manifesto* identifies itself as a communist newspaper philosophically but does not associate with any party and operates as a workers' cooperative. In the nations of the Third World that became independent since World War II, journalism typically was part of freedom movements inherently in support of liberation from colonialism. Many independent publications retain that opposition to entrenched power, such as *The Hindu* in India.

The press in the United States, which was distinctly partisan well into the 19th century, developed objectivity norms that now define the practices of corporate-commercial news media. Many journalists found (and find) those norms constraining, and in the political fervor of the 1960s and 1970s, advocacy journalism emerged with counterculture and revolutionary political activity. Other terms used for practice outside the mainstream include *alternative, gonzo,* or *new* journalism. Within those forms, journalists may openly identify with a group or movement or remain independent while adopting similar values and political positions.

Can those who advocate a particular philosophical or political perspective . . . produce journalism that the general public can trust?

This advocacy-objectivity dichotomy springs from political theory that asserts a special role for journalists in complex democratic societies. Journalists' claims to credibility are based in an assertion of neutrality. They argue for public trust by basing their report of facts, analysis, and opinion on rigorous information gathering. Professional self-monitoring produces what journalists consider an unbiased account of reality, rather than a selective account reflecting a guiding political agenda.

Persuasion vs. Journalism

At one level, the term *advocacy* might be useful in distinguishing, for example, journalistic efforts clearly serving a partisan agenda (such as a political party publication) from those officially serving non-partisan ends (such as a commercial newspaper). But the distinction is not really between forms of journalism as much as between persuasion and journalism. Although so-called objective journalism assumes that, as a rule, disinterested observers tend to produce more reliable reports, a publication advocating a cause might have more accurate information and compelling analysis than a non-partisan one. The intentions of those writing and editing the publication are the key distinguishing factor.

More complex is categorizing different approaches to journalism by those not in the direct service of an organization or movement. Can those who advocate a particular philosophical or political perspective—but remain independent of a partisan group—produce journalism that the general public can trust?

Pilger vs. Burns

An extended example is helpful here. In general usage, freelance reporter John Pilger (Australian born, now living in the United Kingdom) could be considered an advocacy journalist, and *New York Times* reporter, John Burns, an objective journalist. Both are experienced and hard-working, with a sophisticated grasp of world affairs, and both have reported extensively about Iraq. Pilger primarily writes for newspapers and magazines in England but has a large following in the United States, and he also is a documentary filmmaker. Burns writes almost exclusively for the *Times* but also gives frequent interviews on television and radio programs about his reporting. Anti-war and anti-empire groups circulate Pilger's reports and screen his documentaries, but he, like Burns, describes himself as an independent journalist and rejects affiliations with any political groups.

Those who report from the conventional wisdom are not exempt from the questions about perspective.

Pilger is, however, openly critical of U.S. and U.K. policies toward Iraq, including unambiguous denunciations of the self-interested motivations and criminal consequences of state policies. His reporting leads him not only to describe these policies but to offer an analysis that directly challenges the framework of the powerful. Burns, in contrast, avoids such assessments, not only in news reports but also in articles labeled analysis. His reporting tends to accept the framework of the powers promoting these policies, and his criticism tends to question their strategy and tactics, not their basic motivations. In some sense, both journalists advocate for a particular view of state power and how it operates in the areas they cover. Both have reputations for accurately reporting; the difference resides in their interpretations. The language of mainstream journalism would see Burns as objective but not Pilger.

Journalistic Frameworks

The example illustrates the limits of conceptions of journalism as practiced in the media industries, especially those under corporate commercial control. All reporters use a framework of analysis to understand the world and report on it. But reporting containing open references to underlying political assumptions and conclusions seems to engage in advocacy, while the more conventional approach appears neutral. Both are independent, in the sense of not being directed by a party or movement, but neither approach is in fact neutral. One explicitly endorses a political perspective critical of the powerful, while implicitly reinforcing the political perspective of the elite.

Accounts of the world, including journalistic ones, must begin from some assumptions about the way the world works. None is neutral. That doesn't mean there's nothing we can know or trust about the world, or that journalists can't offer us reliable information. It simply means that those who report from the conventional wisdom are not exempt from the questions about perspective.

Readers should keep that in mind. So should journalists.

Journalists Can Be Emotionally Involved in Their Stories

Samuel G. Freedman

Samuel G. Freedman teaches journalism at Columbia University and writes a column for the New York Times. *He is also the author of* Letters to a Young Journalist.

To be a moral journalist, you must retain your humanity. You might think I'm stating the obvious. Yet the ideal of objectivity calls for journalists to be detached from those whom they cover; dispassion is seen as the guarantee of fairness. Personally, I have always thought "objectivity" was the wrong word, anyway, because human beings cannot help but be subjective. What we strive for as journalists is better thought of as fairness. . . . Whether you call it objectivity or fairness or anything else, journalistic distance cannot and should not always override the rest of our nature. Journalism is about channeling emotions, not turning them off. And on some rare and extraordinary occasions it is about tearing down the barrier—what theater people call the "fourth wall"— separating us from the people and events we are reporting. If you can't be a person, then you'll ultimately be less of a journalist.

Two Photographs

The story of two prize-winning photographs and the men who took them goes right to my point. If you've studied the Vietnam War, you've probably come across a photograph of a Vietnamese girl running naked and howling down a road, the victim of a napalm attack by U.S. troops. That single searing

Samuel G. Freedman, *Letters to a Young Journalist*. Cambridge, MA: Basic Books, 2006. Copyright © 2006 by Samuel G. Freedman. Reprinted by permission of Basic Books, a member of Perseus Books, L.L.C.

image played no small part in deepening opposition in the United States to the war, and it also won the Pulitzer Prize for the photojournalist Nick Ut of Associated Press [AP]. What very few people knew was that after Ut finished photographing the girl, Phan Thi Kim Phuc, he brought her onto a minibus, ordered it to a hospital, and pleaded with doctors to attend her right away. Only after Kim Phuc was on the operating table did Ut head to the AP bureau to deliver his film. Twenty-eight years later, in a ceremony before the Queen of England, Kim Phuc said of Ut, "He saved my life." I would add that he also saved his own soul.

The other photo came out of the Sudanese famine in 1993. It caught an emaciated toddler at the moment she collapsed while struggling to reach a feeding station; in the background perched a vulture. Like Nick Ut, Kevin Carter, the freelancer who took the photo, helped to galvanize public opinion with the image. As much as any other single factor, it led President Bill Clinton to deploy the U.S. military on a humanitarian mission in the region. Again like Nick Ut, Carter was honored with the Pulitzer Prize. Unlike Ut, though, he did not intercede to save the subject of his photo. One of Carter's frequent comrades, David Beresford of the British newspaper the *Guardian*, recalled asking him, "What did you do with the baby?" Carter replied, "Nothing, there were thousands of them." (At other times, Carter did say he chased away the vulture and that he cried for hours after taking the photo.) Less than four months after winning the Pulitzer, Carter committed suicide. You can never know the exact thinking of anyone who kills himself or herself, but in the aftermath many of Carter's former colleagues kept thinking about the day he let the journalist in him crowd out the human being.

Covering 9/11

I know how difficult it is for someone . . . new to the profession and trying to acquire the proper temperament, to parse these dueling claims on [his or her] conscience. I know because I was teaching an introductory reporting class at Columbia Journalism School in September 2001. My students were barely a month into their journalistic education on the morning Al Qaeda attacked. Still struggling to learn the most rudimentary techniques, they were instantly hurled into the biggest story since World War II. Unlike some of my faculty colleagues, I didn't send my students down to Ground Zero, fearing for their safety, but I did assign them to report on the aftermath of the attack as part of covering their neighborhood beats around the city. I can say, in retrospect, that the experience made them transcend themselves. They wrote about Dominican-immigrant janitors killed when the Twin Towers collapsed, Sikhs subjected to bias crimes because they were mistaken for Arabs, undertakers preparing stray body parts for burial, the Fire Department bagpipers' band that played hundreds of funerals and memorial services and lost two of its own men.

In the process of reporting those stories, my students also collided with some anguishing and necessary questions. What if someone I'm interviewing cries? Can I touch them? Can I hug them? What if I cry? Am I a bad journalist if I do? My adjunct instructor in the class, Mirta Ojito of *The New York Times*, stepped in to answer. For weeks after the attack, Mirta had been writing for "Portraits in Grief," the *Times* collection of profiles of every identified victim of the Al Qaeda attack. In other words, she was spending virtually every working day interviewing survivors. She told the class about how she had cried over the phone as she spoke with the father of two daughters killed in the Twin Towers. She recalled going into the women's bathroom at the *Times* and finding a colleague there sobbing from the strain. Mirta understood that the tears didn't undermine her as a journalist. To have been unable to feel, and thus to convey, the heartache of those widows and widowers, those parentless children and childless parents—that inhuman remoteness would have been a journalistic failure.

Bagpipe Brothers

One of the students Mirta and I taught that fall was Kerry Sheridan. The articles Kerry did back then about the Fire Department's band led her over the succeeding year to write an exceptional book about the group, *Bagpipe Brothers*. More than most journalists of any age, Kerry was plunged into the ambiguous borderland between journalist and person and was forced to determine both an ethical code and the terms of engagement. She wanted to write a great book and she also wanted to be able to sleep at night. I asked her recently what she would tell [a young journalist]. "In times of tragedy, lines get blurred and the best advice I could give a young journalist on keeping your humanity is to allow yourself to bend with the breeze," she said. "Observe, be content to be in the background, help if you can, but don't make that your priority. Think of how you would feel if your family was in that situation. And carry tissues."

It Is Sometimes Acceptable for Journalists to Help the Subjects of Their Stories

Rachel Smolkin

Rachel Smolkin is managing editor at the American Journalism Review.

A convoy of trucks delivers food to a crowd of starving, frantic people in a Somali village. A famine-relief coordinator turns to you—the reporter—and a photographer. "I'm afraid there'll be a riot if we don't get these trucks unloaded quickly. Could you two please put down your notebook and camera, and help us? It might save a life." What do you do?

The Ethics of Helping

In November 2004, G.D. Gearino, a columnist for the *News & Observer* in Raleigh, [North Carolina,] presented this scenario during a journalism ethics symposium at Washington and Lee University in Lexington, Virginia. A group of professionals, myself included, met with journalism professor Edward Wasserman and his students to debate real and hypothetical ethics quandaries.

The students—and as I recall, they were unanimous— looked surprised at such an easy question. Of course they would help. Why wouldn't they, if they could save lives? One enterprising future reporter even proposed telling her cameraman to shoot footage of her handing out food to the needy.

I was appalled. I informed the students that a journalist's job is to bear witness to history, not participate in it. By pitching in to help, the journalists would compromise their objectivity and insert themselves as actors in a situation they should be chronicling as detached observers.

Rachel Smolkin, "Off the Sidelines," *American Journalism Review*, January 2006. Reproduced by permission of *American Journalism Review*.

Hurricane Katrina

But then Katrina slashed the Gulf Coast, and anarchy gripped New Orleans. Riveting news coverage revealed countless acts of kindness by journalists who handed out food and water to victims, pulled them aboard rescue boats or out of flooded cars, offered them rides to safer ground, lent them cell phones to reassure frantic family members and flagged down doctors and emergency workers to treat them.

These actions humanized reporters and helped give them credibility to challenge the lies and befuddlement of government officials. With a few exceptions, the journalists looked like some of the only responsible adults around.

I began to wonder: Was I wrong, and were the students right?

Does pitching in to help compromise an idealistic notion of "objectivity" but bolster credibility with the public? Is it simply the right thing to do, regardless of the professional ramifications? And is one of our profession's most basic tenets—that journalists shouldn't intervene—needlessly strident, making reporters seem inhuman?

Drawing the Line

"I listened with growing horror as NPR [National Public Radio] attacked the officials trying to aid New Orleans victims, taking an outraged moral high ground," James Lange of Pompano Beach, Florida, wrote to National Public Radio. "We all can see that communications is the main problem: Why did NPR not use its satellite phones and other such gear to help the police communicate? Why did NPR not send in food and water to the convention center? Please, please don't tell me that you refused to help because 'it's not our job.'"

In an online column, NPR Ombudsman Jeffrey Dvorkin shared Lange's comments and those of Mort Cohen of Milwaukee, who called to ask, "Do you ever feel that journalism is an inadequate response to the tragedies you report on?"

"I think this is an issue worth exploring," Dvorkin wrote. "Some in the news business might undoubtedly express astonishment that listeners could be naïve about how journalism sees its obligations. But listeners aren't naïve at all."

The NPR listeners have a point. But if it's OK—even advisable—for journalists to give out food, water or rides after a devastating hurricane, then where's the line between permissible help and unacceptable activism? How do you decide when to shed your observer status and get involved? And do you disclose your participation to readers and viewers, or will that be seen as showboating and only fuel public contempt?

No Easy Answers

Among journalists and ethicists I interviewed for this story, no one took an absolutist stance that journalists should never help under any circumstances. Some seemed deeply conflicted about when to intervene. Others were perfectly comfortable rendering any assistance possible after the hurricane, noting the suffering was so vast that their small contributions hardly altered the outcome of the story.

One reporter who struggled with the question of intervention was the *Washington Post*'s Anne Hull, who is known for her poignant word portraits and wrote one of the most heartrending stories about Katrina's devastation. Her September 3 [2005] piece, "Hitchhiking from Squalor to Anywhere Else," told of Adrienne Picou and her 6-year-old grandson, whom Hull found on an interstate exit ramp. They were "twice homeless: first from the floods and then from the dire conditions of the city Convention Center." Fearing separation, Picou had written near the collar of her grandson's red Spider-Man T-shirt: "Eddie Picou, DOB 10/9/98."

In a telephone conversation and in a subsequent e-mail, Hull both articulated the case against intervention and agonized over that detached role. "I think the human suffering that journalists confronted on Hurricane Katrina was a new experience for many journalists who've not covered wars or foreign countries," she says. "I believe journalists should have an ethical framework to guide them, and in the case of covering catastrophe or hardship, we must try to remember that we are journalists trying to cover a story. That is our role in the world, and if we perform it well, it is an absolutely unique service: helping the world understand something as it happens."

Once you've completed your reporting, 'if you can be of any help in giving assistance, by all means, do it.'

But Hull also felt torn: Adrienne Picou had asked if Hull could take her to Baton Rouge. Hull didn't have a car, but a colleague did. "How can you explain that to somebody, why you can't take them to a shelter?" Hull asks. She told Picou she didn't know when she was going or even where she was sleeping that night.

A Reporter First

In Hull's work, intervention would certainly alter the outcome. "The sorts of stories I do are often different than the broader survey stories that involve a [mixture] of official and human reaction. I usually focus on an individual caught up in a situation, and my role is to document how they figure their way out of it and the feelings that accompany them as they do it."

After she interviewed the Picous, she stepped away and called her editor. She wanted to tell him about the story, but she also was troubled. "I'm struggling here," she told him. "Buck me up; give me a talk." And her editor, Bill Hamilton, reminded her, "You're not an aid worker. You're not a rescue worker."

Throughout her stay in New Orleans, Hull gave away water, PowerBars and wet-naps and let countless people use her cell phone. But she feels that during the course of the reporting "when your notebook is still open and you're still gathering facts, you can't give someone a ride. . . . In terms of taking someone out of New Orleans, rescuing them and taking them to a shelter, that seems to go beyond the line of duty for a journalist."

Even under extraordinary circumstances, we [journalists] have to be very careful to maintain our distance and our independence.

After Hull had said good-bye to the Picous, she was sitting under the interstate typing her story on her laptop when a medic came over to ask directions. "I don't know," she told him. "But see that woman and child over there? She will know, and she needs your help." The medics gave the Picous their first ride in a journey that would wind from a shelter in Northern Louisiana to a cattle ranch in Texas to a new job in Smyrna, Georgia. Once you've completed your reporting, "if you can be of any help in giving assistance, by all means, do it," Hull says.

Staying Objective

Scott Gold, the *Los Angeles Times*' Houston bureau chief, wrote another gripping story from New Orleans. "This city is bleeding," began a front-page September 2 story that ended with Gold crying in his hotel room.

Gold, too, says he's "always been fairly rigid" about intervention and believes journalists derive their credibility in part from their detached-observer status. "I never forgot that ultimately we were there to help the public understand a very turbulent and important and tragic event," he says. "Even under extraordinary circumstances, we have to be very careful to maintain our distance and our independence for the sake of our credibility and the sake of our role in public discourse."

But, he concedes, "I might have softened the edges of that position a bit in New Orleans." Why? "I think the scope of it and the circumstances and the tragedy of it and indeed the sense, particularly in those early days, that it was going to be awhile before help arrived. The things that I was doing, I don't feel like [they] are the kind of things that present great ethical dilemmas."

Gold gave out a little water and offered use of his cell phone. He drove one woman around floodwaters to nearby Charity Hospital. He handed out one 8-ounce bottle of baby formula that his wife had found leftover in their pantry and tucked into a package of supplies. But he felt giving people money or loading evacuees onto boats or planes would have crossed a line. "As much as you may be tempted to do that, you can't," Gold says. "Part of what crosses the line in my mind is the sense that you are seeking to insert yourself into the event and potentially shape it."

'[Journalists] shouldn't be too finicky about the notion that rendering some simple assistance will compromise objectivity.

Other journalists did participate in rescue missions. "I tried to help and when I wasn't needed I took pictures," freelance photographer Marko Georgiev, who was in New Orleans on assignment for the *New York Times*, wrote in a piece for the National Press Photographers Association. Georgiev described helping SWAT officers pull trapped Lower 9th Ward residents into a boat as floodwaters rose. "I tried to stay unbiased and to shoot and cover the story the best way possible. I also tried to help as many people as I could."

But Georgiev was haunted by the despair he had witnessed. "We came to take our trophies and left," the New Jersey-based photographer concluded in his piece. "They have to stay. No place to go. This story will become their lives. Or is it the other way around?" . . .

Ethical Frameworks

The decision to intervene is often made in a matter of seconds, without the luxury of forethought. But ethicists say there is some framework for guiding such choices.

"If journalists becoming a part of the story or an actor in unfolding events gets to be the norm, then the journalistic role is compromised on several levels," says Paul McMasters, the First Amendment ombudsman at the Freedom Forum's First Amendment Center. "One is purely practical. If you are handing out food or engaging in a rescue or that sort of thing, you're not observing; you're not taking notes; you're not seeing the larger picture. Secondly, after a while no matter what your motives, it's going to be interpreted by readers and viewers as grandstanding."

McMasters says that among the factors to consider in deciding whether to intervene is "how natural or instinctive the journalist's impulse is and whether or not there is potential for immediate harm or injury without the journalist's involvement. It is very important that the journalist quickly returns to their professional role as soon as the moment passes." But, he adds, "that's not a very good answer. In the world of journalistic ethics, there are seldom good answers or pat answers."

Michael Josephson, founder and president of the Joseph & Edna Josephson Institute of Ethics in Los Angeles, says the journalist's primary obligation is to act as a human being. "Obviously the more serious it is, if people are in dire straits, the more obligated someone is regardless of who they are to render assistance. The other factor is whether there are others there who can render assistance," he says, noting that simply calling someone over might be sufficient.

"I also think we shouldn't be too finicky about the notion that rendering some simple assistance will compromise objectivity," Josephson adds. "Offering someone a drink of water would be something you'd do if they were in your office." To do otherwise, to withhold simple help in the name of professionalism, "will ultimately discredit the profession in most people's eyes." . . .

Bearing Witness vs. Helping

During the ethics seminar, Wasserman steered the discussion but largely refrained from weighing in. While reporting this story, I called to ask what he thought. "The idea that you would not render aid when it's practical and would be effective is monstrous," he told me.

But Wasserman says help shouldn't be given simply as an emotional reaction when it's not really needed. "Are you in a position to do more good by bearing witness to what you're seeing and, you hope, mobilizing the conscience of large numbers of people to intervene than you are by rolling up your sleeves and helping with a rescue?"

What if your actions alter the story? "Harm averted may not be a story," he replies. "You may have just done yourself out of a story. Oh, too bad. You report it as a first-person [account] or you don't report it at all."

Making the Help Part of the Story

If you do help, should you write about it? Should you show it? . . . Among journalists and ethicists I talked to, the question of when to reveal aid produced the largest split, with some urging full disclosure and others arguing that would constitute self-aggrandizement and generally should be avoided.

The ethics institute's Josephson recommends that reporters who render aid "be very direct about that in the reporting" as a matter of transparency and discuss their actions with editors. "You do it, and let someone else decide whether it kills the story. You don't let somebody drown while you're conducting an internal debate."

He says viewers and readers will decide whether such actions constitute grandstanding. "It is entirely an issue of motive, and people will assess that," he says. "I saw some instances of that, where it looked like just grandstanding. If you're doing it to make the show more grandiose, that's a misuse of people's misery, and it really is quite shameful. If you're not grandstanding and you take the hit, well, that's unfortunate, but the alternative is you let somebody suffer."

Helping or Grandstanding?

But NPR's Dvorkin feels broadcasting acts of kindness "ends up looking, sounding self-serving and manipulative" and shouldn't be part of the story unless it changes the outcome. "If the reporter has affected the outcome of the story by his or her direct involvement, the reporter has an obligation to reveal that."

Bob Woodruff, an anchor and correspondent for ABC News who arrived in New Orleans the Wednesday after the storm hit, calls the detached-observer ideal "a very ivory tower notion that's not practiced in the field."

"We all helped out," he says. Like many others, Woodruff handed out food and water if people asked for it and assisted in other small ways. But he warns: "Never do it and roll on it with your cameras. By definition, if you need to do it, then your cameraman should need to do it as well. . . . The real ones don't shoot it." . . .

Unreported Acts of Kindness

John Roberts, the chief White House correspondent for CBS News, also shied away from broadcasting scenes of him and his colleagues dispensing aid. His crew did shoot one instance in which they threw a line from their boat to a man floating on an inflated bed and towed him to safety. "Out here, every boat is a rescue boat, even ours," Roberts reported on September 5.

While he used that incident to illustrate the devastation, other acts of kindness went unreported. On the eastbound ramp of I-10, he and his crew found a woman in her 70s, horribly dirty, suffering and unable to walk. They took her half a mile up the street so she could seek shade under a broken fire truck. "We weren't into grandstanding," he says. "We didn't want to go on the air and crow about what we were doing."

But some other news organizations "did sort of flaunt what they were doing. It led to some heated e-mail about why didn't we use our helicopters to drop food," Roberts says, noting he and his colleagues didn't receive supplies themselves until five days after the hurricane. "I got e-mail asking, 'How could you be so callous and so cruel as to not help?' The fact is that we were helping; we just weren't telling people." . . .

Your humanity—your ability to empathize with pain and suffering, and your desire to prevent it—does not conflict with [a journalist's] professional standards.

The Special Role of the Media

The Freedom Forum's McMasters believes journalists have done an inadequate job explaining their detached role to the public. "Nobody considers a doctor inhumane who takes a sharp instrument and opens the body of a living human. Nobody thinks they are inhumane because they can engage in that process without getting faint of heart or nauseous," he says. "Journalists step back from the fray to serve humanity on a different level. . . . Yet journalists have been largely incapable of making that point to the American people."

But several journalists interviewed for this story found evidence that Katrina's victims understood they'd come to chronicle their plight—and appreciated that mission.

Peter Slevin, the *Washington Post's* Chicago bureau chief, went first to Biloxi, Mississippi, and then to New Orleans. He was struck by how rarely people asked for help, even though thousands were lining the expressways.

Perhaps, he ventures, people didn't ask because he had only a notebook and pen and not a truck full of water. Or maybe they didn't ask out of self-respect. Or maybe because they figured reporters were there to report and activists were there to dispense aid. "There were times when people I was interviewing said I should get the word out that conditions were miserable, the politicians were absent and, especially, that no one in authority was providing information to the stranded residents," Slevin wrote in an e-mail after we'd talked. "They understood the role and the potential impact of the media." . . .

For me, the images on television and the newspaper work by journalists such as . . . Hull and Gold made the agony so much more real than when we *had pondered ethics* in Wasserman's class that fall morning.

Follow Your Conscience

Here's what I wish I had told his students:

Follow your conscience. Your humanity—your ability to empathize with pain and suffering, and your desire to prevent it—does not conflict with your professional standards. Those impulses make you a better journalist, more attuned to the stories you are tasked with telling. If you change an outcome through responsible and necessary intervention because there's no one else around to help, so be it. Tell your bosses, and when it's essential to a story, tell your readers and viewers, too.

Remember, though, that your primary—and unique—role as a journalist is to bear witness. If you decide to act, do so quickly, then get out of the way. Leave the rescue work to first responders and relief workers whenever possible.

The journalists covering Katrina showed compassion by offering water, rides and rescue, but their most enduring service was to expose the suffering of citizens trapped in hellish shelters and on sweltering interstates, and to document the inexcusable government response.

Without journalists fulfilling that essential role, the resources to help on a larger scale might never have arrived.

The Media Should Not
Remain Neutral When
Reporting on Climate Change

Mark Lynas

Mark Lynas is the author of High Tide: News from a Warming World *and* Six Degrees: Our Future on a Hotter Planet.

Future historians, assuming that there are any, will have an entertaining time looking back at how today's journalists wriggled when confronted with the great moral question of our age. Faced with clear evidence of an existential threat to the survival of the planetary biosphere, news correspondents and media organisations not only constantly fail to convey the true magnitude of the story, but also dash for cover every time the going gets tough.

Journalistic Cowardice

The most sacred principle of news reporting is that of "balance": giving equal weight to both sides of an argument. I say this principle is sacred because it is so little adhered to. Analyse most news journalism and you will quickly discover a welter of unspoken assumptions and hidden biases, from the false parity accorded to the combatants in the Israeli-Palestinian conflict to the refusal to question the "need" for economic growth. The reality, as most journalists will tell you after a couple of drinks, is that "fairness" largely consists of balancing out and accommodating the most powerful lobbies and the loudest voices. In an issue as divisive and politicised as climate change, that for a long time meant according the tiny number of sceptics equal coverage with representatives of the majority scientific consensus, leaving the public woefully misinformed.

Mark Lynas, "Neutrality Is Cowardice," *New Statesman*, vol. 134, September 3, 2007, pp. 20–22. Copyright © 2007 New Statesman, Ltd. Reproduced by permission.

Now it simply means being timid: the reactionary lobby is still powerful enough to shoot down anyone who sticks their head above the parapet and says anything that might vaguely be interpreted as "campaigning".

The spat at [the August 24–26, 2007,] Edinburgh International Television Festival was a classic example of this impulse to timidity. When the anti-environmentalist film-maker Martin Durkin and his Channel 4 commissioning editor Hamish Mykura attacked the BBC's [British Broadcasting Corporation's] upcoming Planet Relief project—a proposed day of climate change-related programming and entertainment modelled on Comic Relief—corporation executives present rushed to disown it. "It is absolutely not the BBC's job to save the planet," insisted News-night editor Peter Barron. "I think there are a lot of people who think that it must be stopped."

> *If more of today's media commentators can summon up the courage to help defend the planet . . . maybe the coming holocaust of global warming can be averted.*

Global Warming and Slavery

If Barron is really suggesting that the BBC should be "neutral" on the question of planetary survival, his absurd stance surely sets a new low for political cowardice in the media. It is also completely inconsistent. On easy moral questions, such as poverty in Africa, the BBC is quite happy to campaign explicitly (as with Comic Relief or Live Aid), despite the claim by the corporation's head of television news, Peter Horrocks, that its role is "giving people information, not leading them or prophesying". By analogy, the BBC would have been neutral on the question of slavery in the mid-19th century, and should be giving full voice today to the likes of the British National Party [a British white supremacist organization]—all in the interests of balance and fairness. Likewise, it should not cover the plight of AIDS orphans in South Africa without constantly acknowledging the views of the tiny minority who still dispute the link between HIV and AIDS.

It is worth re-stating again what a more rigorous and honest approach to climate change might look like. First, it would recognise that, despite small uncertainties regarding the specifics, the larger scientific question regarding causality has been settled for a decade at least. Second, it would acknowledge the moral repercussions of our failure to act so far: on people who are already suffering and dying in more frequent and extreme weather events, on future generations of human beings who will suffer a far worse fate, and on other species that will be driven to extinction as a result.

I recently came across a fascinating academic paper, written by Dr Marc Davidson of the University of Amsterdam and published in the scientific journal Climatic Change, which reviews the striking parallels between arguments made by pro-slavery reactionaries in the US deep south 150 years ago and those made by climate change deniers today. Slave-owners argued that the economic consequences of giving negroes freedom would be disastrous, as the muscles of enslaved Africans were the main energy source of the time, as fossil fuels are today. They also argued that the consequences of abolition were just too uncertain to go through with it. Some even claimed that slavery was good for blacks—as some today argue that more carbon dioxide is "good for us".

Averting Global Warming

With the benefit of historical hindsight, we can see just how false and self-serving the proslavery arguments were. Slave-owners were defending the indefensible, but it took a civil war to end the evil institution they had established. If more of today's media commentators can summon up the courage to help defend the planet, even against the powerful vested interests that continue to profit from its destruction, then maybe the coming holocaust of global warming can be averted without such a deep and bitter conflict.

The Media Should Not Be Neutral in the Debate Between Evolution and Intelligent Design

Chris Mooney and Matthew C. Nisbet

Chris Mooney writes for Seed *magazine and the* American Prospect; *he is also the author of* The Republican War on Science. *Matthew C. Nisbet teaches in the School of Communication at American University.*

On March 14, 2005, *The Washington Post*'s Peter Slevin wrote a front-page story on the battle that is "intensifying across the nation" over the teaching of evolution in public-school science classes. Slevin's lengthy piece took a detailed look at the lobbying, fund-raising, and communications tactics being deployed at the state and local level to undermine evolution. The article placed a particular emphasis on the burgeoning "intelligent design" movement, centered at Seattle's Discovery Institute, whose proponents claim that living things, in all their organized complexity, simply could not have arisen from a mindless and directionless process such as the one so famously described in 1859 by Charles Darwin in his classic, *The Origin of Species.*

Yet Slevin's article conspicuously failed to provide any background information on the theory of evolution, or why it's considered a bedrock of modern scientific knowledge among both scientists who believe in God and those who don't. Indeed, the few defenders of evolution quoted by Slevin were attached to advocacy groups, not research universities; most of the article's focus, meanwhile, was on anti-evolutionists and their strategies. Of the piece's thirty-eight paragraphs, twenty-one were devoted to this "strategy" framing—an emphasis that, not surprisingly, rankled the *Post*'s science reporters. "How is it that *The Washington Post* can run a feature-length [page] A1 story about the battle over the facts of evolution and not devote a single paragraph to what the evidence is for the scientific view of evolution?" protested an internal memo from the paper's science desk that was copied to Michael Getler, the *Post*'s ombudsman. "We do our readers a grave disservice by not telling them. By turning this into a story of dueling talking heads, we add credence to the idea that this is simply a battle of beliefs." Though he called Slevin's piece "lengthy, smart, and very revealing," Getler assigned Slevin a grade of "incomplete" for his work.

Political reporters, generalists, and TV news reporters . . . rarely provide their audiences with any real context about basic evolutionary science.

Renewed Controversy over Evolution

Slevin's incomplete article probably foreshadows what we can expect as evolution continues its climb up the news agenda, driven by a rising number of newsworthy events. In May [2005], for example, came a series of public hearings staged by evolution-theory opponents in Kansas. In Cobb County, Georgia, a lawsuit is pending over anti-evolutionist textbook disclaimers (the case is before the U.S. Court of Appeals for the Eleventh Circuit). And now comes the introduction of intelligent design into the science curriculum of the Dover, Pennsylvania, school district, a move that has triggered a First Amendment lawsuit. . . . President [George W.] Bush and Senator Bill Frist entered the fray when both appeared to endorse the teaching of intelligent design in science classes.

As evolution, driven by such events, shifts out of scientific realms and into political and legal ones, it ceases to be covered by context-oriented science reporters and is instead bounced to political pages, opinion pages, and television news. And all these venues, in their various ways, tend to deemphasize the strong scientific case in favor of evolution and instead lend credence to the notion that a growing "controversy" exists over evolutionary science. This notion may be politically convenient, but it is false.

We reached our conclusions about press coverage after systematically reading through seventeen months of evolution stories in *The New York Times* and *The Washington Post*; daily papers in the local areas embroiled in the evolution debate (including both papers covering Dover, Pennsylvania, the *Atlanta Journal-Constitution*, and the Topeka, Kansas, *Capital-Journal*); and relevant broadcast and cable television news transcripts. Across this coverage, a clear pattern emerges when evolution is an issue: from reporting on newly discovered fossil records of feathered dinosaurs and three-foot humanoids to the latest ideas of theorists such as Richard Dawkins, science writers generally characterize evolution in terms that accurately reflect its firm acceptance in the scientific community. Political reporters, generalists, and TV news reporters and anchors, however, rarely provide their audiences with any real context about basic evolutionary science. Worse, they often provide a springboard for anti-evolutionist criticism of that science, allotting ample quotes and sound bites to Darwin's critics in a quest to achieve "balance." The science is only further distorted on the opinion pages of local newspapers.

Media Circuses

All of this will probably be on full display as the dramatic evolution trial begins in Pennsylvania over intelligent design, or ID. The case, *Kitzmiller v. Dover Area School District*, will be the first ever to test the legality of introducing ID into public-school science classes. The suit was filed by the ACLU [American Civil Liberties Union] on behalf of concerned parents after the local school board voted 6-3 to endorse the following change to the biology curriculum: "Students will be made aware of gaps/problems in Darwin's Theory and of other theories of evolution including, but not limited to, Intelligent Design." The trial is likely to be a media circus. And, unfortunately, there's ample reason to expect that the spectacle will lend an entirely undeserved p.r. [public relations] boost to the carefully honed issue-framing techniques employed by today's anti-evolutionists. . . .

Even the best TV news reporters may be hard-pressed to cover evolution thoroughly and accurately.

In a kind of test run for the Dover trial, the national media decamped to Kansas in May [2005] to cover public hearings over the science curriculum staged by anti-evolutionists on the state school board (hearings that mainstream scientists themselves had boycotted). The event triggered repeated analogies to the Scopes trial[1] (even though there was no actual trial), colorful storytelling themes that described the "battle" between the underdog of intelligent design and establishment science, and televised reporting and commentary that humored the carefully crafted framing devices and arguments of anti-evolutionists.

Even the best TV news reporters may be hard-pressed to cover evolution thoroughly and accurately on a medium that relies so heavily upon images, sound bites, drama, and conflict to keep audiences locked in. These are serious obstacles to conveying scientific complexity. And with its heavy emphasis on talk and debate, cable news is even worse. The adversarial

---

1. Often called the Scopes Monkey Trial, *Scopes v. State of Tennessee* tried a teacher, John Scopes, in 1925 for teaching the theory of evolution and thus breaking a state law prohibiting the teaching of any theory that denied the biblical story of creation. The case was surrounded by the proverbial media circus.

format of most cable news talk shows inherently favors ID's attacks on evolution by making false journalistic "balance" nearly inescapable.

Reporting on Intelligent Design

None of which is to say there aren't some journalists today who are doing a great job with their evolution coverage, and who can provide a helpful model. Cornelia Dean, a science writer at *The New York Times*, presents a leading example of how not only to report on but also how to contextualize the intelligent-design strategy. Consider a June 21 [2005] article in which, after featuring the arguments of an ID proponent who called for teaching about the alleged "controversy" over evolution in public schools, Dean wrote: "In theory, this position— 'teach the controversy'—is one any scientist should support. But mainstream scientists say alternatives to evolution have repeatedly failed the tests of science, and the criticisms have been answered again and again. For scientists, there is no controversy."

The mission of the opinion pages and a faithfulness to scientific accuracy can easily come into conflict.

Besides citing the overwhelming scientific consensus in support of evolution, journalists can also contextualize the claims of ID proponents by applying clear legal precedents. Instead of ritually likening the contemporary intelligent-design debate to the historic Scopes "monkey trial" of 1925, journalists should ask the same questions about ID that more recent court decisions (especially the *McLean v. Arkansas* case) have leveled at previous challenges to evolution: First, is ID religiously motivated and does it feature religious content? In other words, would it violate the separation of church and state if covered in a public school setting? Second, does ID meet the criteria of a scientific theory, and is there strong peer-reviewed evidence in support of it? In short, to better cover evolution, journalists don't merely have to think more like scientists (or science writers). As the evolution issue inevitably shifts into a legal context, they must think more like skeptical jurists.

Evolution on the Op-Ed Pages

And as evolution becomes politicized in state after state through trials and school board maneuverings, it rises to prominence on the opinion pages as well as in news stories. Here, competing arguments about evolution and intelligent design tend to be paired against one another in letters to the editor and sometimes in rival guest op-eds, providing a challenge to editors who want to give voice to alternative ideas yet provide an accurate sense of the state of scientific consensus. The mission of the opinion pages and a faithfulness to scientific accuracy can easily come into conflict.

In fact, these forums are quite easily hijacked by activists. Actors on both sides of the evolution debate, but especially pro-ID strategists, often recruit citizens to write letters and op-eds that emphasize the strategists' talking points and arguments. "You get an awful lot of canned comment on the creation side, which you just can't use," observes William Parkinson, editorial page editor of *The York [Pa.] Dispatch*, one of the two papers closely covering the Dover evolution controversy. Yet despite his awareness of this problem, Parkinson's paper did recently print at least one form letter modeled on a prepared text put out by the American Family Association of Pennsylvania, a Christian conservative group. Precrafted talking points included the following: "This is a science vs. science debate, not a science vs. religion debate—it is scientists looking at the same data and reaching different conclusions." *The York Dispatch*'s rival paper, the *York Daily Record*, printed two letters clearly based on the same talking points.

In our study of media coverage of recent evolution controversies, we homed in on local opinion pages, both because they represent a venue where it's easy to keep score of how the issue is being defined and because we suspected they would reflect a public that is largely misinformed about the scientific basis for the theory of evolution yet itching to fight about it. That's especially so since many opinion-page editors see their role not as gatekeepers of scientific content, but rather as enablers of debate within pluralistic communities—even over matters of science that are usually adjudicated in peer-reviewed journals. Both editorial-page editors of the York papers, for example, emphasized that they try to run every letter they receive that's "fit to print" (essentially meaning that it isn't too lengthy or outright false or libelous).

Dover Debates Evolution

We wanted to measure the whole of opinion writing in these two papers. So for the period of January 2004 through May 2005, we recorded each letter, op-ed, opinion column, and in-house editorial that appeared (using Lexis-Nexis and Factiva databases). We scored the author's position both on the teaching of intelligent design or creationism in public schools and on the question of whether scientific evidence supports anti-evolutionist viewpoints. While this remains a somewhat subjective process, strict scoring rules were followed that would allow a different set of raters to arrive at roughly similar conclusions.

An entirely lopsided debate [on evolution] within the scientific community was transformed into an evenly divided one in the popular arena.

Rather stunningly, we found that the heated political debate in Dover, Pennsylvania, produced a massive response: 168 letters, op-eds, columns, and editorials appearing in the *York*

Daily Record alone over the seventeen-month period analyzed (plus ninety-eight in *The York Dispatch*). A slight plurality of opinion articles at the *Dispatch* (40.9 percent) and the *Daily Record* (45.3 percent) implicitly or explicitly favored teaching ID and/or "creation science" in some form in public schools, while 39.8 percent and 36.3 percent of opinion articles at those two papers favored teaching only evolution. On the question of scientific evidence, more than a third of opinion articles at the two papers contended or suggested that ID and/or "creation science" had scientific support.

In short, an entirely lopsided debate within the scientific community was transformed into an evenly divided one in the popular arena, as local editorial-page editors printed every letter they received that they deemed "fit." At the *York Dispatch* this populism was partly counterbalanced by an editorial voice that took a firm stand in favor of teaching evolution and termed intelligent design the "same old creationist wine in new bottles." *The York Daily Record*, however, was considerably more sheepish in its editorial stance. The paper generally sought to minimize controversy and seemed more willing to criticize Dover school board members who resigned over the decision to introduce intelligent design into the curriculum (asking why they didn't stay and fight) than to rebuke those board members who were responsible for attacking evolution in the first place. When the Dover school board instituted its ID policy in October 2004, the first *York Daily Record* editorial to respond to the development fretted about an "unnecessary and divisive distraction for a district that has other, more pressing educational issues to deal with" but didn't strongly denounce what had happened. "I think we've been highly critical of the personal behavior of some of the board members, but we've tried to be, you know, fair on the issue itself of whether ID should be taught in science class," says the editorial-page editor, Scott Fisher, who adds that the editorial board is "slightly divided" on the issue.

Taking a Stand for Science

Interestingly, however, not all local opinion pages fit the mold of the York papers. Given the turmoil in Cobb County, Georgia, over the introduction of anti-evolutionist textbook disclaimers, the *Atlanta Journal-Constitution* also covered the debate heavily on its opinion pages. But the paper took a very firm stand on the issue, with the editorial-page editor, Cynthia Tucker, declaring in one pro-evolution column that "our science infrastructure is under attack from religious extremists."

Tucker, along with the deputy editorial-page editor, Jay Bookman, also warned repeatedly of the severe negative economic consequences and national ridicule that anti-evolutionism might bring on the community. Meanwhile, a majority of printed letters, op-eds, and editorials in the *Journal-Constitution* (54.2 percent) favored teaching only evolution and argued that ID and/or creationism lacked scientific support (53.5 percent). This may suggest a community with different views than those in Dover, Pennsylvania, or it may suggest a stronger editorial role. (Tucker and Bookman did not respond to queries about whether they print letters according to the proportion of opinion that they receive or use other criteria.) Yet despite the strong stance of the *Journal-Constitution* editorial staff, the editors also actively worked to include at least some balance in perspectives, inviting guest op-eds that countered the strongly pro-evolution editorial position of the paper. Roughly 30 percent of the letters and op-eds to the paper featured pro-ID and/or creationist views.

[News]papers can inform their readers about authoritative scientific opinion without stifling the voices of anti-evolutionists.

At the other local paper we looked at, *The Topeka Capital-Journal*, the issue has not received nearly as thorough an airing, though the proportion of pro-evolution to pro-ID arguments was roughly similar to those in the *Atlanta Journal-Constitution*. Interestingly, the Topeka paper appears to have been somewhat reluctant to go beyond publishing letters on the topic, featuring only two guest op-eds (both in support of evolution) and no in-house editorials or columns. Silence is no way for an editorial page to respond to an evolution controversy in its backyard.

At two elite national papers, *The New York Times* and *The Washington Post*, the opinion pages sided heavily with evolution. But even there a false sense of scientific controversy was arguably abetted when *The New York Times* allowed Michael Behe, the prominent ID proponent, to write a full-length op-ed explaining why his is a "scientific" critique of evolution. And when *USA Today* took a strong stand for evolution on its editorial page ("Intelligent Design Smacks of Creationism by Another Name"), the paper, using its point-counterpoint editorial format, ran an anti-evolution piece with it ("Evolution Lacks Fossil Link"), written by a state senator from Utah, D. Chris Buttars. It was filled with stark misinformation, such as the following sentence: "There is zero scientific fossil evidence that demonstrates organic evolutionary linkage between primates and man." . . .

Covering Evolution Responsibly

So what is a good editor to do about the very real collision between a scientific consensus and a pseudo-scientific movement that opposes the basis of that consensus? At the very least, newspaper editors should think twice about assigning reporters who are fresh to the evolution issue and allowing them to default to the typical strategy frame, carefully balancing "both sides" of the issue in order to file a story on time and get around sorting through the legitimacy of the competing claims. As journalism programs across the country systematically review their curriculums and training methods, the evolution "controversy" provides strong evidence in support of the contention that specialization in journalism education can benefit not only public understanding, but also the integrity of the media. For example, at Ohio State, beyond basic skill training in reporting and editing, students focusing on public-affairs journalism are required to take an introductory course in scientific reasoning. Students can then specialize further by taking advanced courses covering the relationships between science, the media, and society. They are also encouraged to minor in a science-related field.

With training in covering science-related policy disputes on issues ranging from intelligent design to stem-cell research to climate change, journalists are better equipped to make solid independent judgments about credibility, and then pass these interpretations on to readers. The intelligent-design debate is one among a growing number of controversies in which technical complexity, with disputes over "facts," data, and expertise, has altered the political battleground. The traditional generalist correspondent will be hard-pressed to cover these topics in any other format than the strategy frame, balancing arguments while narrowly focusing on the implications for who's ahead and who's behind in the contest to decide policy. If news editors fail to recognize the growing demand for journalists with specialized expertise and backgrounds who can get beyond this form of writing, the news media risk losing their ability to serve as important watchdogs over society's institutions.

When it comes to opinion pages, meanwhile, there's certainly more room for dissent because of the nature of the forum—but that doesn't mean editorial-page editors can't act as responsible gatekeepers. Unlike the timidity of the *York Daily Record* and *The Topeka Capital-Journal*, *The York Dispatch* and *The Atlanta Journal-Constitution* serve as examples of how papers can inform their readers about authoritative scientific opinion without stifling the voices of anti-evolutionists.

One thing, above all, is clear: a full-fledged national debate has been reawakened over an issue that once seemed settled. This new fight may not simmer down again until the U.S. Supreme Court is forced (for the third time) to weigh in. In these circumstances, the media have a profound responsibility—to the public, and to knowledge itself.

Organizations to Contact

The editors have compiled the following list of organizations concerned with the issues debated in this book. The descriptions are derived from materials provided by the organizations. All have publications or information available for interested readers. The list was compiled on the date of publication of the present volume; the information provided here may change. Be aware that many organizations take several weeks or longer to respond to inquiries, so allow as much time as possible.

Accuracy in Media (AIM)
4455 Connecticut Ave. NW, Suite 330
Washington, DC 20008
(202) 364-4401 • fax: (202) 364-4098
e-mail: info@aim.org
Web site: www.aim.org

AIM is a conservative watchdog group that criticizes liberal bias in the media. The group monitors the news media for biased or inaccurate stories and publishes critiques of these stories. These critiques can be found in AIM's twice-monthly newsletter, a syndicated weekly newspaper column, and a number of reports, briefings and columns that appear on AIM's Web site.

Center for Media Literacy (CML)
23852 Pacific Coast Hwy., #472, Malibu, CA 90265
(310) 456-1225 • fax: (310) 456-0020
e-mail: cml@medialit.org
Web site: www.medialit.org

CML promotes media literacy—the ability to access, understand, analyze, and evaluate information in the media. CML promotes the teaching of media literacy in schools through advocacy and teacher training. *Connect* is the periodical newsletter of the organization, and archives of the magazine *Media & Values* (1977–1993) are available on the CML Web site.

Committee of Concerned Journalists

National Press Bldg., Washington, DC 20045
(202) 662-7155
e-mail: ccj@concernedjournalists.org
Web site: www.concernedjournalists.org

The Committee of Concerned Journalists works to strengthen journalism's future by advocating for the core principles and functions of journalism. The committee holds workshops for reporters and conducts research. Its publications include the book, *The Elements of Journalism: What Newspeople Should Know and the Public Should Expect*, and a collection of tools for journalists, students, and citizens, which are available on its Web site.

Fairness and Accuracy in Reporting (FAIR)

112 W. Twenty-seventh St., New York, NY 10001
(212) 633-6700 • fax: (212) 727-7668
e-mail: fair@fair.org
Web site: www.fair.org

FAIR is a national media watchdog group that criticizes media bias and censorship. It believes that the media are controlled by, and support, corporate and governmental interests and that they are insensitive to women, labor, minorities, and other special-interest groups. It publishes the bimonthly magazine *Extra!*

Media Awareness Network (MNet)

1500 Merivale Rd., 3rd Fl.
Ottawa, ON K2E 6Z5 Canada
(613) 224-7721 • fax: (613) 224-1958
e-mail: info@media-awareness.ca
Web site: www.media-awareness.ca

The goal of MNet is to promote and support media education in Canadian schools, homes, and communities through a Web site. The site encourages critical thinking about media information and about such issues as media stereotyping. MNet's publications include *Making Your Voice Heard: A Media Toolkit for Youth* and *Exploring Media & Race.*

Media Research Center (MRC)

325 S. Patrick St., Alexandria, VA   22314
(703) 683-9733 • fax: (703) 683-9736
e-mail: mrc@mediaresearch.org
Web site: www.mrc.org

MRC is a conservative media watchdog organization that documents and fights against liberal bias in the news and entertainment media. It gathers and publicizes examples of media bias on its Web site and through its other publications, which include the weekly *Media Reality Check* and the biweekly *Notable Quotables.*

National Association of Black Journalists

8701-A Adelphi Rd., Adelphi, MD   20783-1716
(301) 445-7100 • fax: (301) 445-7101
e-mail: nabj@nabj.org
Web site: www.nabj.org

Founded in 1975, the National Association of Black Journalists serves to strengthen ties among African American journalists, promote diversity in newsrooms, and honor the achievements of black journalists. It publishes the *NABJ Journal* ten times a year.

Poynter Institute

801 Third St. South, St. Petersburg, FL   33701
toll-free: (888) 769-6837
Web site: www.poynter.org

The Poynter Institute exists to provide training and instruction to practicing journalists, journalism students, and professors of journalism. Encouraging ethical journalism is one of the institute's major focuses. Archives of "Everyday Ethics" and "Talk About Ethics" columns, as well as tip sheets for ethical reporting, can be found on the institute's Web site.

Reporters Committee for Freedom of the Press

1101 Wilson Blvd., Suite 1100, Arlington, VA   22209
(703) 807-2100
e-mail: rcfp@rcfp.org
Web site: www.rcfp.org

The Reporters Committee for Freedom of the Press was
founded in 1970 to help journalists fight subpoenas that would
require them to disclose their confidential sources. The committee maintains a hotline for journalists needing legal advice
and advocates in legal cases related to the freedom of the
press. It publishes the quarterly magazine *News Media & The
Law*, as well as a number of pamphlets and handbooks that
catalog the laws protecting journalists.

Society of Professional Journalists

3909 N. Meridian St., Indianapolis, IN   46208
(317) 927-8000 • fax: (317) 920-4789
Web site: www.spj.org

The Society of Professional Journalists is dedicated to encouraging the free practice of journalism and stimulating high
standards of ethical behavior. It provides professional development opportunities for journalists and advocates for the freedom of the press. Its publications include the bimonthly *Quill
Online* magazine, the annual *Journalist* magazine, and an annual Pulliam/Kilgore Freedom of Information report.

Bibliography

Books

Thomas Bivens   *Mixed Media: Moral Distinctions in Advertising, Public Relations, and Journalism*. Mahwah, NJ: Lawrence Erlbaum, 2004.

Elliot D. Cohen   *News Incorporated: Corporate Media Ownership and Its Threat to Democracy*. Amherst, NY: Prometheus, 2005.

Nicholas Davies   *Flat Earth News: An Award-Winning Reporter Exposes Falsehood, Distortion and Propaganda in the Global Media*. London: Chatto & Windus, 2008.

Howard Good   *Desperately Seeking Ethics: A Guide to Media Conduct*. Lanham, MD: Scarecrow, 2003.

Tony Harcup   *The Ethical Journalist*, Thousand Oaks, CA: Sage, 2007.

Neil Henry   *American Carnival: Journalism Under Siege in an Age of New Media*. Berkeley and Los Angeles: University of California Press, 2007.

Dale Jacquette   *Journalistic Ethics: Moral Responsibility in the Media*. Upper Saddle River, NJ: Pearson Prentice Hall, 2007.

Eric Klinenberg   *Fighting for Air: The Battle to Control America's Media*. New York: Metropolitan, 2007.

Stephanie Greco Larson
Media and Minorities: The Politics of Race in News and Entertainment. Lanham, MD: Rowman & Littlefield, 2006.

Philippe Perebinossoff
Real-World Media Ethics: Inside the Broadcast and Entertainment Industries. Boston: Elsevier, 2008.

Benjamin Radford
Media Mythmakers: How Journalists, Activists, and Advertisers Mislead Us. Amherst, NY: Prometheus, 2003.

Arundhati Roy
An Ordinary Person's Guide to Empire. Cambridge, MA: South End, 2004.

Roger Simpson and William Coté
Covering Violence: A Guide to Ethical Reporting About Victims and Trauma. New York: Columbia University Press, 2006.

Graham Spencer
The Media and Peace: From Vietnam to the "War on Terror." Basingstoke, UK: Palgrave Macmillan, 2005.

Tom Wheeler
Phototruth or Photofiction? Ethics and Media Imagery in the Digital Age. Mahwah, NJ: Lawrence Erlbaum, 2002.

Lee Wilkins and Renita Coleman
The Moral Media: How Journalists Reason About Ethics. Mahwah, NJ: Lawrence Erlbaum, 2005.

Periodicals

G. Stuart Adam, Stephanie Craft, and Elliot D. Cohen	"Three Essays on Journalism and Virtue," *Journal of Mass Media Ethics*, vol. 19, no. 3/4, 2004.
Eric Alterman	"Fool Me Once . . . ," *Nation*, January 23, 2006.
Eric Alterman	"It Ain't Necessarily So . . . ," *Nation*, September 10, 2007.
Brian Cathcart	"Our World of Rough-and-Ready Ethics," *New Statesman*, September 10, 2007.
Tim Cavanaugh	"Cartoons Make Cowards of Us All," *Reason*, May 2006.
Communication World	"Is Paying for Media Coverage Ever Ethical?" November-December 2006.
Brent Cunningham	"Re-thinking Objectivity," *Columbia Journalism Review*, July-August 2003.
Sally Dadisman	"Naming Names," *American Journalism Review*, June-July, 2007.
Deryl Davis	"The Rest of the Story," *Sojourners*, November 2004.
Geri L. Dreiling	"Threats of Jail," *National Catholic Reporter*, December 17, 2004.
Jared Flesher	"Between Right and Wrong," *Columbia Journalism Review*, January-February 2006.

Edward Greenspon — "To Be Terrified of the Word Is to Give in to the Terrorists," *Globe and Mail* (Toronto), September 18, 2004.

Deborah Howell — "Quote, Unquote," *Washington Post*, August 12, 2007.

Deborah Howell — "A Dilemma Within Quotation Marks," *Washington Post*, August 19, 2007.

Tom Jicha — "Lacrosse Players Didn't Get Fair Shot in National Media," *South Florida Sun-Sentinel*, October 30, 2006.

Leslie Kemeny — "Radiation, Terrorism and the Media," *Quadrant*, January-February, 2006.

John Lanchester — "Riots, Terrorism Etc.," *London Review of Books*, March 6, 2008.

Jeff Lee — "Prof. Says Media Fuelling School Shootings," *Montreal Gazette*, October 3, 2006.

Mark Lisheron — "Lying to Get the Truth," *American Journalism Review*, October-November 2007.

Douglas McCollam — "The Shame Game," *Columbia Journalism Review*, January-February, 2007.

Kelly McParland — "Call Them the Terrorists They Are," *National Post*, September 25, 2004.

Raymond T. Odierno	"The Photograph of a Dying Soldier," *New York Times*, February 3, 2007.
Tom Plate	"Finding the Balance Between Patriotism and Proper Journalism Is Not Always Easy," *San Diego Business Journal*, July 24, 2006.
Daniel Pipes	"They're Terrorists—Not 'Activists' or 'Victims,'" *National Post*, September 7, 2004.
Bill Saporito	"When to Give Up a Source," *Time*, July 11, 2005.
Gabriel Schoenfeld	"A License to Leak," *Weekly Standard*, October 22, 2007.
Ted Vaden	"Tricky Issue: Naming Sex Case Accusers," *Raleigh (NC) News & Observer*, January 28, 2007.
Joan Voight	"Realistic or Offensive? Advertising Leans on Stereotypes. When Do They Cross the Line?" *Adweek*, September 1, 2003.
Wall Street Journal	"Fit and Unfit to Print," June 30, 2006.
Don Wycliff	"Publishing Pictures That Might Offend," *Chicago Tribune*, September 9, 2004.

Index